NIGHT

OUT

LONDON

THE COMPLETE OPEN-AIR GUIDE

SARAH BROWN

A Nicholson Guide

Nicholson an imprint of
Bartholomew a division of
HarperCollins*Publishers*

© Sarah Elizabeth Brown Ltd 1991

London Underground Map by
permission of London Regional Transport

Illustrations by Tamsin Hickson
Design by Bob Vickers
General map by Martin Brown. © Nicholson 1991
Park maps by Rodney Paull. © Nicholson 1991

Nicholson
HarperCollins*Publishers*
77-85 Fulham Palace Road
Hammersmith
London W6 8JB

Printed and bound in Great Britain by
Scotprint Ltd, Musselburgh

ISBN 0 7028 1257 9

91/1/110

CONTENTS

OPEN SPACES IN LONDON

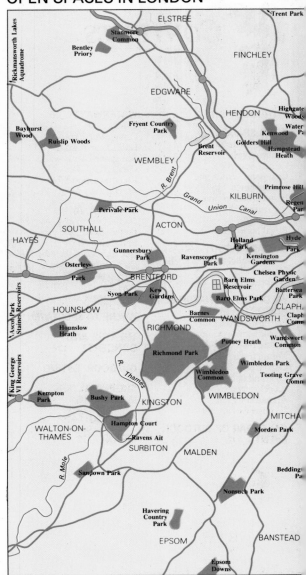

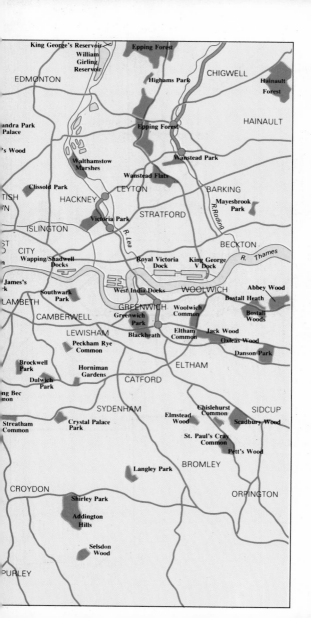

UNDERGROUND

Travel Information 071-222-1234
Travelcheck 071-222-1200

Interchange stations
Connections with British Rail
Connections within walking distance
Closed Sundays
Closed Saturdays and Sundays
Served by Piccadilly Line early mornings and late evenings (by Metropolitan at other times)
For opening times see poster journey planners
Certain stations are closed during public holidays

Diary 10 150mm x 76mm 3/90

Key to lines

Bakerloo
Central
Circle
District
East London
Hammersmith & City
Jubilee
Metropolitan
Northern
Piccadilly
Victoria

Docklands Light Railway
Network SouthEast

Restricted service
Restricted service
Peak and Sunday mornings
Peak hours only
Peak hours only
Peak hours only
Under construction

© Copyright London Regional Transport

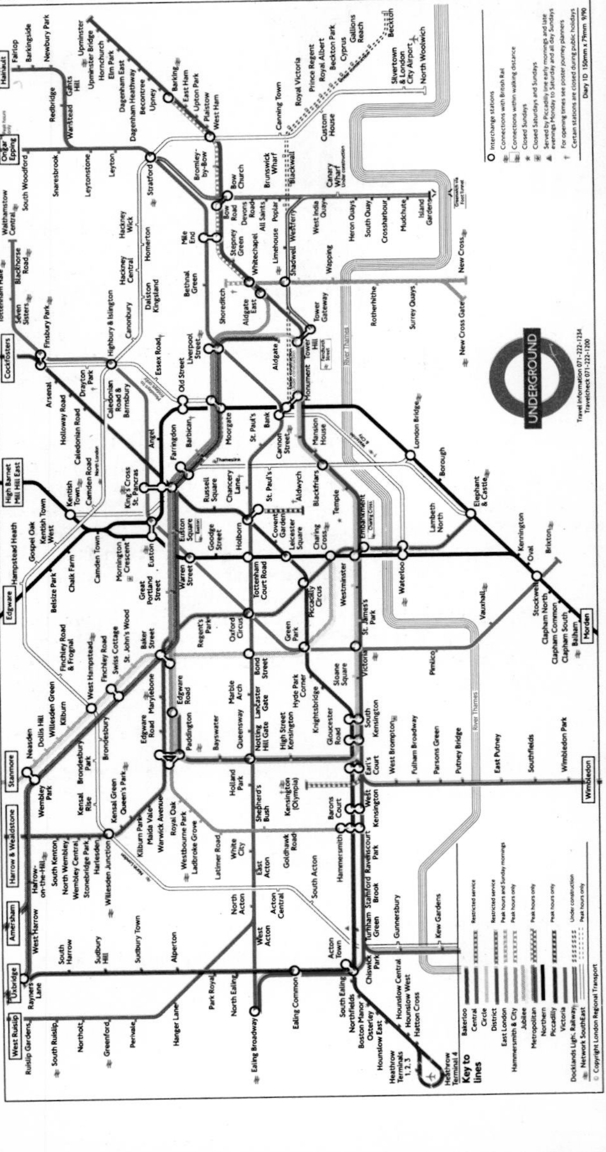

INTRODUCTION

I WROTE this book whilst living in Central London. I do find it remarkable how much varied outdoor activity is virtually on the doorstep. Did you know it was possible to go parascending on Wanstead Flats? Orienteering on Hampstead Heath? Dragonboat racing on the Thames? You can become a zoo volunteer; join an archaeological dig in the heart of the city; put on wellies and help with tree planting without leaving the capital; tour historic districts; take a river trip to the eighth Wonder of the World. All these are just a selection of what is on offer out and about in London.

I began discovering London's great outdoors when I took up the sport of orienteering. This interest led me to many parks and woodlands, heaths and commons in the London area. There are over 4000 open spaces here ranging from the huge expanses of Richmond Park to the tiny Camley Street Natural Park. I have also found out about other less well-known spaces which are fun to discover, for example the intriguing canal system and fascinating Victorian cemeteries.

If you enjoy being out and about, this book will tell you what there is to do, where to find it and how to get there. There's something for everyone, whether you are interested in sport, wildlife and natural history, or conservation and archaeology. You might prefer to sit back and spectate. If so, there's plenty to choose from, with eccentric English activities such as Swan Upping to the sporting classics of Wimbledon and the Derby.

A calendar of outdoor events makes it easy to see what is on throughout the year and there are details of the main sporting events, their venues and how to get tickets.

On a more edifying note, there are open-air theatres and venues for concerts, and numerous outdoor eating places, including pubs, restaurants and picnic spots.

I hope this book will inspire you to reach out and make the most of some of these nearby facilities, whatever the weather!

Sarah Brown London 1991

Acknowledgements

Thanks to everyone I met and spoke to in connection with this book who gave me much useful information.

I am also grateful to my editorial team of Louise Cavanagh and Sarah Hudson for their help and to my agent Harriet Cruickshank.

Thanks to my husband, Paul Street for his encouragement and to my baby son, Ralph, whose long periods of sleep enabled me to get on with my writing.

Sarah Brown

OPEN SPACES

LONDON is fortunate to have retained an enormous number of open spaces. They range in character from the bracken-covered slopes and uncultivated grassland of Richmond Park, where deer roam in large numbers, to the manicured gardens of Regent's Park. There are pockets of woodland, commons, walled gardens, wild flower meadows and landscaped lawns once only enjoyed by the wealthy. These spaces, nearly 2000 in Greater London, attract a wide variety of wildlife as well as being show-cases for fine specimens of native and exotic trees and glorious floral displays. Many of the larger spaces provide additional facilities such as bowling, boating, tennis and tree trails. You'll even come across wallabies, herons, dinosaurs and deer.

It is impossible to include every open space but I've selected a variety that all have something special to offer.

Botanic gardens

The most famous of these gardens is Kew, but it is well worth seeking out the others. Although smaller, they have plenty of interest and also provide tranquillity in the midst of London.

Avery Hill
Bexley Road, Eltham SE9
081-850 2666
This winter garden, a Kew in miniature, has an appealing dilapidated air. It was built in 1890 by Colonel North as a place for his family to exercise in inclement weather. A walk round the vast glass house in sub-tropical temperatures surrounded by jungle-like vegetation makes you forget the murkiest February day. Don't miss the weird staghorn fern almost hidden in one corner. In the summer, the secluded formal gardens to the side of the conservatory are ablaze with colour. The rest of the park is quite plain, with a good view of London's southern suburbs.
Open: 13.00-18.00 (to 16.00 in winter) Mon-Fri, 07.00-dusk (or 21.00) Sat & Sun.
Free
BR: Falconwood, Eltham Park

Chelsea Physic Garden
Royal Hospital Road SW3
071-352 5646
This physic garden was founded in 1673 for the collection, study

and dissemination of plants that have medicinal value. Botanical research is still carried on here. The four acres are divided into a multitude of small areas each with a specific collection of plants. My favourite sections are the culinary and medicinal beds where the smoking tobacco plant nestles under a giant sunflower, and there are many interesting vegetables such as sea kale and cardoon. You can learn the difference between hemlock (poisonous) and sweet cecily which could be useful on a foraging trip to the countryside! In the gardens is the oldest 'purpose-built' rockery made from Icelandic lava and rubble from the Tower of London. There are many fine trees including the largest olive tree in Britain.

Open: Apr-Oct 14.00-17.00 Wed & Sun.
Charge
Tube: Sloane Square

Fulham Palace Grounds & Botanic Garden

Bishop's Avenue SW6
071-736 7181
By a curious coincidence, a long line of bishops who lived at Fulham Palace were keen gardeners and they developed the reputation of this small area in horticultural circles. The best known - Bishop Grindal - was in Queen Elizabeth I's reign. He is reputed to have planted the first tamarisk tree in Britain and used to send a selection of fruits from the garden to tempt the royal palate. The lawns and trees around the palace buildings are very attractive, peaceful and dog-free. There are occasional guided walks around the grounds. Near the gatehouse is a special playground run by the Handicapped Adventure Playground Association (HAPA) 071-731 2753.

Adjacent to the Palace grounds is Bishops Park with facilities including a boating lake and paddling pool, bowling green, tennis courts, putting green and sandpit. Along the River Thames is a delightful walk lined with impressive sycamore trees.

Open: Botanic Garden: 09.00-dusk Mon-Sun; Bishops Park: 07.30-dusk Mon-Sun.
Free
Tube: Putney Bridge

Museum of Garden History

St Mary-at-Lambeth, Lambeth Road SE1
071-261 1891
This 17th-century Botanical garden was founded at St Mary-at-Lambeth church by the Tradescants, father and son. As gardeners to Charles I and Henrietta Maria, they brought many rare plants into this country, some of which can be seen in the churchyard.

Open: 11.00-15.00 Mon-Fri, 10.30-17.00 Sun.
Free
Tube/BR: Waterloo

Royal Botanic Gardens, Kew
Kew Road, Richmond, Surrey
081-940 1171
The Botanic Garden at Kew was started in 1759 with a small area devoted to botanic collections. The garden today has been greatly extended and there are numerous different features to enjoy. There is a splendid collection of trees from the English Oak to the striking Tulip tree; woodland, grass and aquatic gardens, rockery and rhododendron dell. More exotic plants and trees are housed in the magnificent glass houses, The Palm House and the Temperate House, designed by Decimus Burton. You can climb up to the

Royal Botanic Gardens, Kew

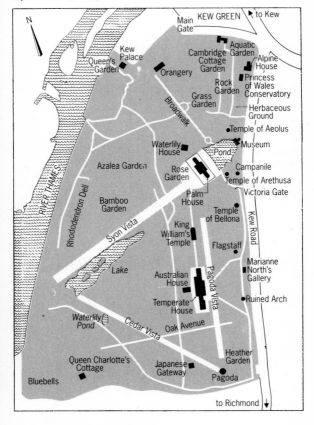

gallery for a panoramic view of the jungle of greenery below. Inside the new Princess of Wales Conservatory are fascinating displays including Living Stones (Lithops), the Giant Waterlily, weird and wonderful cacti, and hungry carnivorous plants. If Kew is one of those places that you've always meant to visit, do go. It is most rewarding.

Open: Gardens: 09.30-closing time varies from 16.00-18.30 Mon-Sat and from 16.00-20.00 Sun (phone to check). Glasshouses: *10.00-16.00 Mon-Sat, to 17.30 Sun.*
Charge
Tube/BR: Kew Gardens, *BR:* Kew Bridge

South Lambeth Botanical Institute
323 Norwood Road, Herne Hill SE24
081-674 5787
This is a small, formal Botanic Garden specialising in certain groups of plants such as Rubus (blackberries and raspberries) of which they have many wild species, and Umbelliferae, including two species of Giant Hogweed. The family Polygonaceae is also grown here which includes docks and rhubarbs, of local interest as it was in this part of London that cultivated varieties of these plants were first raised.
Open: 09.00-16.00 Mon (all other times by appointment only).
Free (donations appreciated)
BR: Tulse Hill, Herne Hill

Windsor Great Park (Savill Gardens)
Windsor, Berkshire
(0753) 860222. An outstanding woodland garden created in the 1930s by Sir Eric Savill in the grounds of Windsor Castle. It covers 35 acres and includes large collections of roses, herbaceous plants and alpines. There is also a lake.
Open: Mar-Dec 10.00-19.00 (or dusk) Mon-Sun.
Charge
BR: Windsor

Country parks

Country parks differ from other parks in that they are managed specifically with a view to conserving the landscape and the flora and fauna as well as providing recreational facilities for the public. Within or just on the boundary of the Greater London Area there are seven such parks, and a further dozen or so in the Green Belt.

Bayhurst Wood Country Park
Brakespear Road North, Harefield, Buckinghamshire
(0895) 630078 (Park Office)
(0895) 50111 ex 2450 (Hillingdon Leisure Service)
There are 100 acres of mature oak and hornbeam to enjoy at Bayhurst Wood Country Park, and a further 900 acres just nearby

which includes Ruislip Woods. Facilities include a barbecue area, horse riding, and way-marked nature trail for which a leaflet is available from the park office. Also at the park office you can get details of the guided walks. There is a café here for teas on summer Sundays (April-October).

Open: dawn-dusk Mon-Sun.
Free
Tube: Ruislip

Colne Valley Park
Denham Court, Village Road, Denham, Buckinghamshire
(0895) 832662
This park was conceived as a regional park in the 1960s and provides a real taste of the countryside on London's western doorstep. Much of the area is privately owned but there is plenty of access for the public and a variety of activities on offer such as riding, boating, swimming, sailing and miles of footpaths and bridleways. The park is 14 miles long, extending from Rickmansworth to Staines, and covers over 40 square miles. Just west of the M25 are Black Park and Langley Park with hundreds of acres of woodland, nature reserve, rhododendron garden and arboretum.

For details of all the activities, tours, walks, and how to get involved with the conservation work, phone the park office.

Fryent Country Park
Fryent Way, Kingsbury NW9
081-900 5038
Hell Lane is the name of the ancient trackway that goes through part of this country park. There are more than 300 acres of woodland, hay meadows, open spaces, old ponds and hedgerows dating back to medieval times, and a picnic site. The variety of habitats encourage a good range of wildlife with unusual butterflies, birds and insects and over 100 species of wild flowers. For details of

guided walks and other activities here, contact the park ranger on the above number.
Open: 24 hrs Mon-Sun.
Free
Tube: Kingsbury, Wembley Park

Hainault Forest Country Park

Romford Road, Chigwell, Essex
081-500 7353
This 900-acre country park includes over 300 acres of ancient pollarded hornbeam wood. There are ample paths and three miles of bridleways making exploration easy on foot or horseback. Much of the rest of the area is undulating grassland suitable for picnics, kiteflying, winter sports or sunbathing according to the season. During the summer there are organised activities each week including guided walks, conservation days and festivals. Phone the park office for details.
Open: 07.00-dusk Mon-Sun.
Free
Tube: Hainault (then by bus 62)

Havering Country Park

Pinewood Road, Havering-atte-Bower, Essex
(0708) 720858
Once part of a Royal Estate, these 165 acres consist of mature woodland, glades and meadows crossed by a network of paths and horse rides with fine views over London and the Essex countryside. Thanks to Victorian landscaping, there are over 100 magnificent Wellingtonia or Redwood trees in the park. Facilities include two picnic sites, a way-marked circular walk of about one hour, and an events programme of guided walks (shared with Hornchurch Country Park) which offers intriguing titles such as a Fungus Foray, Mini-beast Hunt for Children and a *04.30* start for catching the dawn chorus. Details of these are available from the park office.
Open: 08.00-½hr before dusk Mon-Sun.
Free
BR: Romford (then by bus 165, 294)

Hornchurch Country Park

Albyns Farm Lane, off Southend Road, Hornchurch, Essex
(Main Car Park: Squadrons Approach, Hornchurch, Essex)
(04027) 54451
260 acres of new woodland, only planted in 1980, make up part of this park, as well as lakes, open spaces and the Ingerbourne Valley Marsh which is a Site of Special Scientific Interest (SSSI). Facilities include a trim trail, fishing lake (permit needed), two picnic areas, and bird watching from converted bunkers which look across the marshes. They share a programme of guided walks with Havering

Country Park (see above). For details of these, phone the park office (at Albyns Farm on above number) for the leaflet.

Open: Apr-Oct 08.00-21.30 Mon-Sun; Nov-Mar dawn-dusk Mon-Sun.

Free

Tube: Elm Park, Hornchurch *BR:* Romford

Horton Country Park

Epsom, Surrey

(Car Park: West Park Farm, Horton Lane, Epsom)

(0372) 726252 or (0372) 741191 (answerphone)

Horton, a word that meant muddy or dirty place, was the name given to the original medieval settlement in the area. Don't let that put you off as there are now over 200 acres of country park to enjoy here including a mixture of woodland, grassland, ponds and hedgerows with a huge variety of wildlife. There are plenty of footpaths, way-marked tracks for riders, an information centre, and a picnic area with barbecue facilities plus a programme of walks and activities throughout the year.

Open: 24 hrs Mon-Sun.

Free

BR: Epsom

Lee Valley Regional Park

Lee Valley Countryside Centre, Abbey Farmhouse, Crooked Mile, Waltham Abbey, Essex

(0992) 713838

The Lee Valley Park stretches north from Stratford in London's East End nearly 30 miles into Hertfordshire near Ware. Over 20 different outdoor activities take place here including many different sports on land and water as well as numerous countryside pursuits. Within the area of the park are a number of bird and nature reserves, farms, country park areas and gardens. For information on the countryside activities contact the countryside centre.

There is a large programme of walks, some of which are aimed specifically at children, some for the family. These last between 2-2½ hours and cover subjects such as finding out about trees and wild flowers, bats and spiders, exploring the many water courses and old railway lines. They also run day-long events in water-colour painting, photography, bird-watching and boat trips.

If you feel like organising your own trip there are some very clear leaflets on a number of circular walks that have been created here, as well as a good booklet on where to go bird-watching. The area certainly lives up to its promise of having something for everyone.

Open: Park: *most of the countryside sites are open dawn-dusk Mon-Sun;* Countryside Centre: *Apr-Oct 10.00-17.00 Mon-Sun; Nov-Mar phone for details.*
Charge
BR: Waltham Cross

South Norwood Country Park
Albert Road, Croydon, Surrey
081-760 5584
Part of this 120-acre park is a conservation area, with a special wetland habitat and secluded island for breeding birds. There is also a recreation ground, with adventure playground and trim trail with 12 activities to keep you fit whilst enjoying the woods and wild flower meadows.
Open: 24 hrs Mon-Sun.
Free
BR: Woodside, Penge

Trent Park Country Park
Cockfosters Road, Enfield, Hertfordshire
081-449 8706
Once part of the Royal Hunting Forest of Enfield Chase, this country park consists of 413 acres of grasslands, woodland and lakes. There is also a water garden, nature trail and picnic areas. In the part known as Church Wood there is a special trail for blind or partially-sighted people. A tapping rail is provided from the

main entrance on Cockfosters Road and braille notices describe some of the scenery and items that can be touched.
Open: 07.30-½ hr before sunset Mon-Sun.
Free
Tube: Cockfosters, Oakwood

Cemeteries

The cemeteries around London provide a fascinating insight into Victorian attitudes with their impressive and often idiosyncratic monuments. Apart from historical interest, these places have become peaceful sanctuaries for wildlife.

Highgate Cemetery
Swain's Lane N6
081-340 1834
Now the best known of London's cemeteries, it was opened by the London Cemetery Company in 1839 on the southern side of Highgate West Hill. The grounds were laid out by an architect and civil engineer who created winding paths amongst mature trees leading up to The Egyptian Avenue and Circle of Lebanon. This was built around the magnificent Cedar of Lebanon which dominates the cemetery today. Even in Victorian times, Highgate cemetery was a tourist attraction as it was a fashionable place to be (either dead or alive!) and there are many famous 'residents' including George Eliot, Kate Greenaway, Marie Lloyd, Lord Lister and Philip Harben (the first TV cook). An extension was opened to the east of Swain's Lane, and a hydraulic system and tunnel were constructed so that coffins could go from the chapel in the west to burial in the east without leaving consecrated ground. The 'Friends of Highgate Cemetery' was founded in 1975 and they have endeavoured to protect and restore the site whilst leaving much of the prolific undergrowth and wild flowers that give the place so much atmosphere. Guided tours, highly recommended, are on offer round the beautiful older western section.
Open: The eastern cemetery: *Easter-end Oct 10.00-17.00 Mon-Sun; Nov-Easter 10.00-16.00 Mon-Sun (closed during funerals):* The western cemetery: *by guided tour only - phone for details.*
Charge
Tube: Highgate

Kensal Green Cemetery
Harrow Road W10
081-969 0152
This was the first of the great commercial cemeteries of London. Thanks to a couple of early royal burials (the Duke of Sussex, sixth son of George III and his sister Sophia) it became a fashionable place to be laid to rest. There are plenty of monuments to admire, and many mature native trees lining the curving avenues. Famous tombs include Isambard Kingdom Brunel, William

Thackeray, Charles Blondin (the tight-rope walker) and James Miranda Barry – Inspector General of the Army Medical Department who on death was found to be a woman.

Open: 09.00-17.30 Mon-Sat, 10.00-17.30 Sun & 10.00-13.00 Bank holidays.

Free

Tube/BR: Kensal Green

Nunhead Cemetery

Linden Grove SE15

071-639 1613 (Friends of Nunhead Cemetery - *evenings and week-ends)*

In its heyday, this was one of the seven important cemeteries built in a ring around London. Of the 30-40,000 monuments, one of the most famous was a memorial to the five Scottish martyrs who were transported in 1793 for campaigning for Parliamentary reform. By the middle of the 20th century, the cemetery had fallen into disrepair and many of the graves and monuments had been vandalised.

Very few burials take place here now, but this overgrown undulating site is now an important wildlife sanctuary. There are a wide range of habitats, unusual in such an urbanised area, which attract a number of breeding birds, foxes, bats and squirrels. In addition to the wild flowers, there are remnants of the botanical planting that was carried out in Victorian times. Much of the area is going wild but a small part is managed by the Friends of Nunhead Cemetery. They run guided tours at *14.15* on the last Sunday of every month, and hold practical work days on the first Sunday of every month.

Open: 14.00-16.00 Wed, 10.00-16.00 Sat & Sun.

Free

BR: Nunhead

Commons, heaths and woodlands

Whilst parks and gardens are pleasant places, most have a certain manicured feel that links them inextricably with city life. London has other open spaces which, whilst managed, are left in wild natural states. These are the woods, heaths and commons of which a surprising number have survived. The larger of these open spaces, such as Hampstead Heath, Wimbledon Common and Epping Forest, are well known, but numerous smaller areas are just as rewarding to explore. I've selected a range of my favourites, most of which I have got to know through orienteering events.

SSSI's

Sites of Special Scientific Interest (SSSI's) are designated so by the Nature Conservancy Council in order to preserve some of the best examples of a particular type of landscape or geological feature. There are some 36 of these sites in the greater London area, many of which are accessible to the general public. There are very good examples of ancient woodland at Epping Forest and Oxleas Wood, chalk downland near Croydon, grazing marshes along the Thames estuary, and reservoirs where waterfowl can breed and winter.

Other sites include: Barnes Common, Hainault Forest, Hampstead Heath, Ruislip Woods, Stanmore Common and Bentley Priory, Walthamstow Marshes, Wimbledon Common.

Addington Hills, Croydon, Surrey

This small area consists of a mass of steep, wooded valleys gouged out of the hill leading up to a grassy plateau dominated by a tall monument. The intricate lie of the land gives children lots of opportunity to rush or slither down the slopes and find hiding places in the many hollows. There are plenty of footpaths and bridle-tracks for the more sedate. Near by, and within easy reach of Addington Woods, is Lloyd Park, a small parkland area with a good expanse of open grassland and some pleasant meadows.

Facilities include a café.

Barnes Common SW13

This common was once used by the men of Barnes and Putney to graze their animals until a dispute meant the men of Barnes refused to let the Putney animals near the place! The most animosity you get now is the tooting of horns as the area is criss-crossed by several major roads, a bottle neck in the rush hour. Despite the traffic, the place has a certain wildness with the bright flowering gorse and broom amongst the clumps of trees and many wild flowers.

Facilities include a permanent orienteering course, picnic space.

Bostall Heath & Woods SE2 and Lesnes Abbey Woods SE2
081-311 1674/310 2777

These two areas, separated only by the A206, make up one of South London's largest patches of woodland. Lesnes Abbey takes its name from the 12th-century abbey that lies in ruins here. Steep ridges and valleys run from north to south making it quite physical to go cross-country but there are some well-defined paths to make exploration easy. Good views over the Thames Estuary are to be had. A good time to visit is the spring when nearly 20 acres of the woods are ankle-deep in wild daffodils.

Facilities include a bowling green, cricket practice nets and a permanent orienteering course and camping near by.

Epping Forest
Epping Conservation Centre, High Beach, Loughton, Essex
081-508 7714

Epping Forest is the remains of a primaeval forest that stretched from the Thames north to the Wash and east to the Essex coast. Just over 100 years ago, it was whittled away to 3000 acres and its existence came under threat. The Corporation of the City of

London stepped in, won a court battle, saved the forest and a further 3000 acres which were deemed to have been illegally enclosed. Today the Corporation manage this marvellous belt of forest and are duty bound to keep it open to the public. It is about six miles long and two miles wide. There are numerous paths and bridletracks through the forest. These can be heavy going in the winter with the mud churned up by horses and in the summer they dry out to leave treacherous ruts. It is best to head off into the forest proper. Though easy to get lost, you are never too far from a major path and junction. The woods are lovely with much hornbeam and beech undulating over dells and slight hills. There are patches of thick undergrowth and several streams and ponds. Although the whole area is called Epping Forest, about one third is open grassland.

There is a conservation centre that gives information on the forest, and organises courses and guided walks. Another way to get to know the woods thoroughly is to do the 15-mile centenary walk (see page 42). There is also a wheelchair path for the disabled to explore some of the forest.

Facilities include: fishing, golf course, horse riding.

Hampstead Heath NW3
including Kenwood, Parliament Hill, Golders Hill Park, West Heath, Sandy Heath and Hill Gardens.
071-485 4491/081-455 5183
Hampstead Heath, just four miles from the centre of London, feels remarkably like 'real countryside'. It's a wonderful place to explore with plenty of contrasts, hidden-away corners, attractive grassy slopes, wild flower meadows, woodland walks, secluded ponds and spacious lakes.

The most popular parts are around Kenwood House, where the lawns slope steeply to the lakes and concert area, and Parliament Hill, a superb viewing point for London and a favourite spot for kite flying. To the side of the hill are chains of ponds used variously for swimming, boating, fishing and as bird reserves.

It is worth getting to know other areas of the heath. Just the other side of Spaniard's Road is Sandy Heath, a pretty piece of woodland with a remote peaceful atmosphere. The undulating ground slopes down to the Heath Extension, a rather ugly name for a large chunk of open land ending up in the heart of Hampstead Garden Suburb. It's a short walk to Golders Hill Park with its flamingoes, deer and animal enclosure, and charming flower garden. From here, you can walk up through the shady woods of West Heath towards Jack Straw's Castle. On one side is a delightful garden called The Hill on which stands a romantic pergola with crumbling pillars and ivy-covered balustrades. Quite unlike anywhere else and worth seeking out.

Facilities include: Parliament Hill: athletics track, bowling green, cricket, football and hockey pitches, netball and tennis courts, lido, open-air pools, orienteering course, paddling pool and sand-pit. Golders Hill Park: putting green, tennis courts, deer and animal enclosure. Heath Extension: cricket, football and rugby pitches, cricket nets, horse riding.

Hampstead Heath

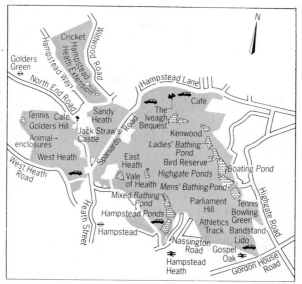

Highgate Woods and Queens Woods N6

These two small patches of woodland, once part of a great forest covering Middlesex, are sandwiched between Alexandra Palace and Hampstead Heath. Both have a good number of tarmac paths running through but these don't detract from the pleasant wood-land. Highgate Woods have a more open feel, and more forest flowers including foxgloves and anemones. In Queen's Wood, the vegetation is denser and the ground slopes quite steeply leading down to two secluded pools on the valley floor.

Hounslow Common, Middlesex

This large common on the western edge of London was once a hide-out for highwaymen and footpads; now it is a significant nature reserve. The main part of the common is a mixture of gorse, broom, blackberry and hawthorn, with 20 acres of alder woodland. The River Crane runs through part of the area, and these river banks, designated an SSSI, are some of the few surviving natural river banks left in London. Apart from the flora and fauna, the area attracts many butterflies and species of bird.

Oxleas Wood, Castle Wood, Jackwood and Shepherdleas Woods SE18

Together these woods make up one of the largest woodland areas in south-east London and feature on the Green Chain Walk (see page 42). Oxleas and Shepherdleas survive from ancient woodland whose origins can be traced back to the Ice Age. Such woods, increasingly rare, attract a different sort of wildlife from less mature forests. The area is criss-crossed by a number of paths and the vegetation is fairly dense. There are a great number of different trees including the wild service tree, many woodland flowers and fungi as well as a variety of breeding birds.

The area rises to a ridge where there are fine views across a large grassy space. To the west, where the ground slopes steeply, is Severndroog Castle. It is a triangular 18th-century folly, named after the Castle of Severndroog on the Malabar coast which was successfully defended against pirates. This spot still has a touch of romance with views over London and a beautiful rose garden.

Chislehurst and St Paul's Cray Commons with Pett's Wood and Scadbury Park, Kent

These two commons, mainly wood and grassland, are bordered by the Scadbury Park Nature Reserve to the east and an extensive

stretch of National Trust land to the south which includes Pett's Wood. The whole area, with its variety of habitats, is rich in wildlife. Bromley Council produce nature trail leaflets for both the commons and Scadbury Park.

The commons, open heath some hundred years ago, are now mainly woodland with oak and birch. Gravel extraction left a legacy of ponds which attract aquatic and marsh plants as well as butterflies and Mallard and Canada geese. The ancient grassland that survives on Chislehurst Common is one of the most important features. Best seen in June and look out for harebells in late summer.

In contrast to the ancient commons, Scadbury has only been a nature reserve since 1985, though the estate has been in existence since Saxon times and there are mature oak trees from the Tudor period. There are damp areas of alder woods with moisture-loving plants such as the marsh marigold and bluebell. The ponds are inhabited by dragonflies, newts and frogs. Parts of the reserve have chalk- and lime-based soils attracting a different type of vegetation.

To the south is Pett's Wood, bought by public subscription in 1927, containing a granite sundial, an appropriate memorial to the founder of British Summer Time and Chislehurst resident, William Willet. These are pretty woods with birch, oak and some chestnut crossed by a number of footpaths and bridle-tracks.

Ruislip Woods, Ruislip

These woods, adjacent to Bayhurst Wood Country Park, combine an important ecological site with a popular recreation area. The predominant leisure feature is the 40-acre lake which comes complete with its own sandy beach. It was dug originally to provide water for the Grand Union Canal but is now home to a variety of watersports. The woods which extend from the water's edge are one of the best surviving examples of coppiced hornbeam. They are designated an SSSI because of this and the rich variety of fungi, forest flowers, trees and shrubs found here. There are plenty of footpaths and bridle-paths through the area.

Stanmore Common and Bentley Priory, Middlesex

If you are a fungus fan, you should make a trip here. Both areas have several damp boggy parts in which a tremendous range of fungi flourishes. At Stanmore Common nearly 300 species have been identified which is why it has been categorised an SSSI. Stanmore Common is somewhat of a misnomer as it is almost entirely wooded and densely so at that. There's a good path network, well-trodden by numerous dog walkers who frequent the area. There are one or two open spaces amongst the woods as well as a cricket pitch. One part of the area comprises a mass of tree-covered humps and hollows, a legacy from the gravel digging that once took place here.

Bentley Priory, although adjacent, has quite a different character. It is mostly open land pockmarked with patches of very dense scrub rather like small copses. The land slopes up from Boot Lake (a boot of the thigh-high variety) where there is also a bird sanctuary. You may glimpse deer on a neighbouring piece of private parkland.

Wimbledon Common SW19
081-788 7655

Wimbledon is mostly associated with tennis and immaculate lawns, so this large, wild area comes as rather a surprise. There are open grassy areas crossed by wide tracks and bridle-paths, as well as thick, brambly woodland which is quite steep in parts. Amongst the trees are several secluded lakes and in the centre, next to the car park, is the only example of a hollow post wind-mill, now a museum illustrating the development of windmills.

Historic houses and gardens

Many of London's more interesting open spaces were once gardens and country estates of the nobility. Now, overtaken by the advance of urban London, they still provide an escape from the bustle of traffic. More than this, many of these gardens give a sense of magic as you enter domains that were once the preserve of the very wealthy. Several of the ones I've chosen to describe have kept something of the richness of their original designs.

Brockwell Park SE24
081-674 6141

Once the home of a wealthy glass maker, Brockwell Park was opened to the public nearly 100 years ago. There are extensive views from the hill, where the mansion stands, to the south of the park and to an attractive chain of ornamental lakes to the west. Near one of the lakes is a delightful walled garden created at the beginning of this century, the first of its kind in a London park. Of the original topiary, a large yew arch still exists and there are colourful formal beds to enjoy.

   Facilities include: bowling green, children's paddling pool, cricket pitches, open-air swimming pool, netball and tennis courts. *Open: Mar-Oct 06.30-dusk Mon-Sun; Nov-Feb 07.30-dusk Mon-Sun.*
Free
BR: Herne Hill

Cannizaro Park
West Side, Wimbledon SW19
081-946 7349

It is easy to overlook this little gem as it nestles so close to the vast open spaces of Wimbledon Common and Richmond Park. It is a delight from when you first walk up the formal entrance way flanked by attractive flower beds opening onto a pretty fountain. Round the corner there's a sloping lawn with many lovely trees, woods and a hint of walled garden to lead you further on. The park is small enough to explore every corner. There is a water garden, azalea dell, formal rose garden and spacious kitchen garden surrounded by balustrades. Woodland walks lead back round to Cannizaro House (now a hotel and a good place for a luxury afternoon tea) where there is a pretty sunken garden with paved walks and stone-edged beds.

Open: dawn-dusk Mon-Sun.
Free
Tube/BR: Wimbledon

Chiswick House

Burlington Lane, Chiswick W4
081-994 3299

The gardens surrounding this striking house are stunning and of much interest to anyone keen on garden history. These are among the earliest examples of the English landscaped garden when designers broke with formal Dutch traditions. Formal and natural elements are blended together with a sculptured lake, 'ruined' cascade and pretty bridges, all manner of statuary and architectural features with obelisks, a temple and columns.

A fashionable feature of the period was the Patte D'Oie or Goose Foot - radiating avenues in the shape of a webbed foot. In between, trees and shrubs were planted at random with small meandering paths contrasting with the formal avenues. The effect works just as well today. One minute you can be walking along a hedge-lined

Chiswick House

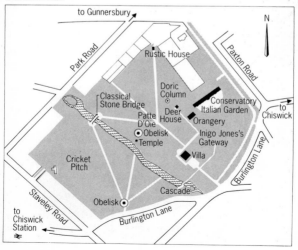

path towards a Doric column, but turn the corner and there is a feeling of natural woodland. Interesting vistas and tranquil corners make it easy to forget London's arteries pulsing just outside.

Facilities include a cricket ground and refreshment pavilion.

Open: Gardens: *dawn-dusk Mon-Sun;* House: *mid Mar-mid Oct 09.30-13.00 & 14.00-18.30 Mon-Sun; mid Oct-mid Mar 09.30-13.00 & 14.00-16.00 Wed-Sun.*
Gardens: free; House (English Heritage): charge
Tube: Turnham Green   *BR:* Chiswick

Clissold Park N16
071-254 9736
The history and naming of Clissold Park could be straight out of a romantic novel. It was once the home of the Crawshays. One of the daughters fell in love with the local vicar, the Reverend Clissold, a liaison which didn't meet with papa's approval. The couple managed a secret correspondence but had to wait until the old man died to marry. Whereupon the Reverend renamed the estate Clissold's Place or Park.

There are many mature trees here which survive from the original estate as well as two ornamental lakes which attract bird life. There are also deer and a miniature zoo, as well as an aviary.

Facilities include: bowling green, children's playground and paddling pool, football pitch, netball and tennis courts, running track,
Open: 07.00-dusk Mon-Sun.
Free
Tube: Manor House

Danson Park
Danson Road, Bexleyheath, Kent
081-303 7777
Much of the present park was landscaped by Capability Brown. Ambitious water schemes often featured in his designs and this

was no exception. He damned the Danson stream, flooded the site of the original mansion and created a 20-acre boating lake which is the predominant feature today. It is now a major leisure facility. There are some other attractive smaller features especially the rockery, heather and water gardens.

Facilities include: bowling green, children's playground, tennis courts and on the lake: canoeing, rowing and paddle-boat hire, sailing and windsurfing.

Open: Apr-Oct 08.30-dusk Mon-Sun; Nov-Mar 07.30-16.30 Mon-Fri, 09.00-16.30 Sat & Sun.

Free

BR: Welling, Bexleyheath

Ham House

Ham, Richmond, Surrey

081-940 1950

Ham House (owned by the National Trust) and gardens have a magnificent setting on the banks of the River Thames. The rural surroundings accentuate the formality of the gardens. To the east of the house is the Principal or Cherry garden which is a masterpiece of design. The formal beds bordered by miniature hedges are a mixture of ordinary lavender whose spiky flowers give a misty blue air and pale green-grey cotton lavender pruned in perfect hemispheres, grouped close together so the ground seems to undulate. It is the most remarkable sight.

Behind the house are some plain lawns leading to 'The Wilderness', a geometric feature of radiating trees and hedges enclosing small grassy areas. To the west is a pretty rose garden and stables, now a tea-room with refreshments served on the spacious lawns whenever possible in the spring and summer.

Open: 10.00-18.00 Tue-Sun.

Free

Tube/BR: Richmond (then by bus 71)

Holland Park W8

071-602 2226

From Kensington High Street, first impressions of Holland Park are that it is somewhat ordinary – a shaded avenue leading to a large open area for sports and picnicking, but persevere. Once the private 'garden' of Holland House, there are some charming formal gardens and secluded woods at the top of the hill. A section of these was once an arboretum and certain features such as Lime Tree Walk and Chestnut Walk remain. Now secondary woodland has developed and is being managed ecologically so that the habitat for the 50 or so species of birds and numerous mammals will be improved. Patient bird lovers may well see the tawny owl, greater- and lesser-spotted woodpecker and fly catcher, species not normally associated with city life, not to mention a collection of peacocks, peafowl and pheasants. An authentic Japanese garden is being constructed in time for Japanese year in 1992.

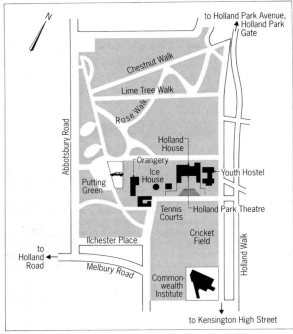

Holland Park

Facilities include: adventure playground, cricket pitch and nets, golf nets, football, open-air theatre, putting green, tennis courts.
Open: 08.00-sunset Mon-Sun.
Free
Tube: Holland Park, Kensington High Street

Horniman Gardens
100 London Road, Forest Hill SE23
081-699 2339
The museum here attracts plenty of visitors with its eccentric collection of artefacts, but take time to enjoy the gardens too. There are good views over to St Paul's just by the bandstand. My favourite section is the secluded water garden with its numerous pools that cascade down by the lace-like wrought iron conservatory.
Facilities include: small children's zoo, open-air concerts.
Open: 08.00-dusk Mon-Sun.
Free
BR: Forest Hill

Osterley Park

Isleworth, Middlesex
081-560 3918

This park and house is owned by the National Trust. There are 140 acres of parkland consisting of broad lawns, and a group of lakes bordered by ancient cedar trees. The most striking feature of the park is the house, an elegant red-brick mansion with stunning interiors.

Open: Park: *10.00-20.00 (or sunset) Mon-Sun;* House: *11.00-17.00 Tue-Sun.*
Park: free, House: charge
Tube: Osterley   *BR:* Thornbury Road

Syon Park

Park Road, Brentford, Middlesex
081-560 0881

The main gardens surround the lake, a natural-looking feature which was dug out to the specifications of Capability Brown – he ordered a million cubic feet of soil to be removed. The lake-side shores are planted with weeping willow and swamp cypresses, and in the spring are carpeted with daffodils.

The conservatory just by the entrance is absolutely charming with its great central dome and elegant curving wings embracing a pretty formal garden. Come here in late spring and early summer for the beautiful magnolia trees with their huge strongly scented blossoms.

Syon Park is said to be the first place where trees were planted purely for ornament and there are many interesting species in the woodland gardens. Formal bedding areas and lawns surrounding Flora's Column (the Roman Goddess of flowers) give a blaze of summer colour, whilst pink and crimson ericas in the heather bed light up any winter gloom.

Open: 10.00-dusk *Mon-Sun.*
Charge
Tube: Gunnersbury   *BR:* Syon Lane

Wanstead Park

Blake Hall Road E11
081-508 2266

Visit Wanstead Park for its remarkable lakes and attractive woodland. The estate was mainly developed by Sir Richard Child who wanted to create a Hampton Court in East London. His house, demolished in 1824, didn't ever have such grand dimensions but the 1½ mile chain of lakes is impressive to this day. The woods surrounding the lakes are a mixture of oak and sycamore with elm, silver birch and beech. The area has a number of footpaths and some rough grassland in the southern part.

Open: dawn-dusk *Mon-Sun.*
Free
Tube: Wanstead   *BR:* Manor Park

Waterlow Park N6
071-272 2825

Sir Sydney Waterlow gave this park to the public in 1889 to act as a 'garden for the gardenless'. Situated on a steep hillside with an unusual three level lake, there are charming formal gardens, shrubberies and terraces. At the top of the hill is a weather vane which is supposed to be on the same level as the top of St Paul's Cathedral. Within the park is Lauderdale House, a grade 1 listed building which was gutted by a fire in 1963. Some of the house has been restored and there is a lively community arts programme. More funds are needed to finish the work.

Facilities include; children's play area, putting green, restaurant, tennis courts.

Open: 07.30-dusk Mon-Sun.
Free
Tube: Highgate

Parks

The first public park was opened in 1845 with the aim of giving the overcrowded East End a bit of breathing space. It proved a popular idea; today there are a great many parks, still with their first aim being to provide open space for densely populated areas. Gone are some of the public baths and open-air pools but there are often extensive sports facilities and good places to eat (see section on Eating Out).

Alexandra Park & Palace N22
081-444 7696

Having orienteered here frequently, I feel as though I know every corner. From the palace itself (now an exhibition and leisure centre) there are good views of London. Grassy slopes with small copses lead down to the flat open area that was once a racecourse. Tucked away in the south-east corner is a small wildlife pond area well-stocked with reeds and bullrushes. For a good walk, take the path to the west over Muswell Hill Road along the old railway track into Highgate Woods. Circle back to 'Ally Pally' via Queen's Woods.

Facilities include: boating lake, pitch and putt, animal enclosure and children's playground.

Open: 24 hrs Mon-Sun.
Free
Tube: Wood Green   *BR:* Alexandra Palace

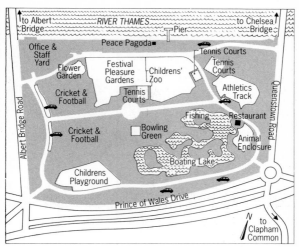

Battersea Park

Battersea Park SW11

081-871 7530

These 200 acres were reclaimed from Thames marshland and opened by Queen Victoria as a public park in 1858. Many original features still exist such as the Ornamental Lake and a variety of formal gardens. In 1951, the Festival Pleasure Gardens were laid out to celebrate the Festival of Britain. Modern additions include the magnificent Peace Pagoda which was built by the Bhuddist order, Nipponzan Myohoji, and completed in 1985. There is also a two-acre nature reserve.

Facilities include: athletics track, bowling green, children's zoo and animal enclosure, cricket and football pitch, tennis courts.
Open: dawn-dusk Mon-Sun.
Free
Tube: Sloane Square   *BR:* Battersea Park, Queenstown Road

Crystal Palace SE20

081-778 7148

Crystal Palace, with its spouting fountains and special prehistoric monsters, was a Victorian forerunner to today's Disney-style parks. The monsters survive and they are probably top of the list of the many features that make this such an appealing park for children today. There is a zoo, a mini-fair, pony and trap, and mini steam train. The maze, still surrounded by the original ring of trees from the 1890s, has recently been reinstated.

Facilities include: boating and fishing lake, cricket pitch, orien-

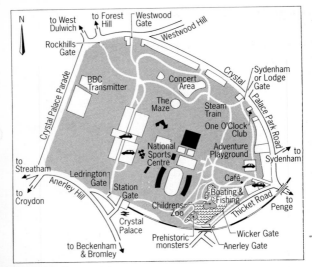

Crystal Palace

teering course. For details of the main sporting facilities see Crystal Palace Sports Centre on page 131.

Open: 08.00-½ hour before dusk Mon-Sun.
Free
BR: Crystal Palace

Dulwich Park SE21

081-693 5737

It is best to come here in May and June to get the full glory of the rhododendron and azalea gardens which were a favourite of Queen Mary, wife of George V. If you are keen on trees, Dulwich Park boasts a marvellous range of species from old oaks and other native British trees to exotics such as Japanese pagoda tree, tree of heaven, and Kentucky coffee tree. Trees that were damaged in the recent storms are being replaced. There are two tree trails and leaflets (minimal charge) are available from the park office.

Two ecological areas in the park are planted with indigenous species that will in turn attract indigenous wildlife. Another special feature of the park are 'touch' maps that have been developed for the blind and coloured maps for the visually handicapped.

Facilities include: boating lake, bowling green, children's playground, café, cricket pitch and nets, football pitches, putting green, tennis courts.

Open: Jun, Jul & Aug 08.00-21.00 Mon-Sun; all other times 08.00-16.30 Mon-Sun.
Free
BR: North Dulwich, West Dulwich

Dulwich Park

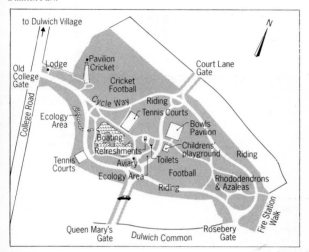

Ravenscourt Park W6
071-736 7181
This tiny park is tucked in between busy Goldhawk Road and King Street but it does have the merit of its own tube station! Despite the size, there are a number of interesting features. The islanded lake is rich in birdlife and there is a special scented garden for the visually handicapped. This is an old feature of the park which is being improved with many new aromatic plants and foliage. The old stables used to be one of my favourite vegetarian eating places. Under new management the menu is now more mixed but the setting is just as attractive.

Facilities include: chlorinated paddling pool, putting green, red gra (hard surface area for kick about), tennis courts.
Open: Mar-Oct 07.30-dusk Mon-Sun; Nov-Feb 07.30-17.00 Mon-Sun.
Free
Tube: Ravenscourt Park

Victoria Park E9
081-985 1957
Affectionately known as 'Vicky Park' by the locals, this is the

oldest of the public parks designed by James Pennethorne (who also laid out Battersea Park). The original lakes are still here as is the splendid drinking fountain built in 1871. The park makes a good starting point if you want to do a canal walk along either Regent's Canal or the Hertford Union, both of which run close by.

Facilities include: athletics arena, bowling green, children's playground and deer pen, cricket and football pitches, netball court.

Open: Mar-Oct 06.00-dusk Mon-Sun; Nov-Feb 06.00-16.30 Mon-Sun.

Free

BR: Cambridge Heath

Royal parks

Ten London parks belong to the Crown and are administered by the Department of the Environment. They make up only a small percentage of London's open spaces but are probably the best known green areas. Although all royal, these parks are not at all uniform. Each has a very different character and all are worth getting to know.

Green Park and St James's Park SW1
071-930 1793

These two welcome green spaces in the heart of London's West End are surrounded by some of the capital's best known streets – The Mall, Horse Guard's Parade, Piccadilly and Pall Mall. Tourists are far outnumbered by office workers at lunchtime as the parks act as a garden for the surrounding buildings. You might be hard-pushed to spot a space between the striped deckchairs and striped suits.

St James's is the older of the two parks acquired in 1532 by Henry VIII who drained the marshes and turfed out the lepers. Charles II opened it to the public and created many of the features that remain today, such as Pall Mall and Birdcage Walk. This once lived up to its name as it was lined with cages of parrots and other

ornamental fowl. St James's has a refined, yet friendly feel, and whilst the open space is enjoyable you can't forget that you are in the heart of London.

Green Park, to the west, lives up to its name as there is little else here but trees – lime, plane and hawthorn, and lawns. It is a shady place to stroll and makes a good escape from the endless traffic in Piccadilly.

Open: dawn-dusk Mon-Sun.
Free
Tube: Green Park, St James's Park

Greenwich Park SE10

081-858 2608

A boat trip down river from the centre of London is the ideal way to arrive at Greenwich and the park. On the top of the hill is the Old Royal Observatory with its pretty outline. From here gaze down over the river to the misty horizons of the docklands and in the foreground the elegant Queen's House designed in 1619 by Inigo Jones. Don't forget to stand astride the zero meridian to get one foot in each hemisphere – east and west that is. There are some delightful formal gardens further along the hill, with glorious floral displays in spring and summer as well as a lake and numerous fine trees. Quieter than the apron of ground in front of the Observatory, this is a lovely place to explore. Hidden away here is the Wilderness where the park's herd of deer is kept. The two viewing points are easy to miss (as are the deer!)

Behind Greenwich Park is Blackheath, a bare stretch of land edged with attractive town houses. It has been a rallying point throughout history from Roman times to the Peasants' Revolt. Modern invaders are thousands of runners preparing to start the London Marathon which takes place each spring.

Facilities include: boating pool, children's playground, cricket pitches, deer park, rugby pitch, tennis courts.

Open: Mar-Oct 07.00-22.00 Mon-Sun; Nov-Feb 07.00-18.00 (or dusk) Mon-Sun.
Free
DLR: Island Gardens (then by foot tunnel) *BR:* Greenwich

Hampton Court and Bushy Park, Middlesex

081-977 8441

These parks, nestling in a loop of the Thames, have one of the most attractive settings in London. The maze is probably the most famous feature of Hampton Court gardens. There's a giddy sense of relief when you get out but a feeling of achievement if you get to the middle and back. Near the maze are some pretty flower beds and an arboretum, but the most stunning part is to the rear of the palace. Charles II, a lover of the formal gardens of the French, wanted Hampton Court to be the English version of Versailles. As a result the Long Water, an impressive canal ¾ of a mile long, was constructed. It is surrounded by formal avenues of ornamental yew trees, once tiny cones, which have been pruned to resemble giant spinning tops.

On the other side of the palace are the formal Tudor gardens, some sunken and hemmed in by mellow walls of old brick. The Great Vine, over 200 years old, is housed here, and in a good year produces some 700lb of fruit which goes on sale in late summer.

Across Hampton Court Road, near the maze, is Bushy Park. It seems very expansive and spacious after the enclosed formality of Hampton Court. The main feature is Chestnut Avenue, a wide road running through the centre of the park, at its best in May when the blossom is out in full. To the east of the avenue are a series of ponds and to the west the Woodland Gardens, watered by an artificial stream and planted with masses of azaleas and rhododendrons and many interesting trees. Fewer people get this far from the palace so it's possible to find some secluded spots.

Open: 07.45-dusk Mon-Sun.

Free

BR: Teddington, Kingston, Hampton Wick

Hyde Park W1 and **Kensington Gardens** W8
071-262 5484

Hyde Park is the place for rallies, festivals and fireworks. It has a history of being a park for the people, starting with the first lot let in by Charles I. He also created the Ring which became a very fashionable carriage drive.

The most dominant feature is the Serpentine, as the name suggests, a sinuous lake created originally from six ponds. The lake is used for swimming, boating and fishing (with a permit and the

Hyde Park and Kensington Gardens

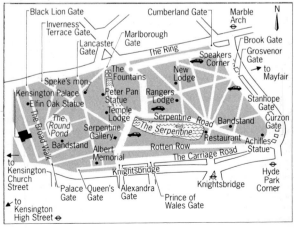

understanding that as long as anything is caught it is put back alive). The lake shores are crowded with deckchairs and picnickers in good weather, and devoted runners and joggers from dawn till dusk. In the summer too, the main areas of open space to the east are a mass of games with softball, cricket, football, and frisbee. Although there is a lot of activity, the slight undulations to the west where there are more trees provide some pleasant quieter spots for those just wanting relaxation.

Over the road is Kensington Gardens which has quite a different feel. The gardens were separated from Hyde Park by Queen Caroline who had the tree-lined avenues constructed in 1730, intending the space for her own recreation. Luckily public access was never entirely lost, though nothing so rowdy as football or public meetings are allowed here. There is a children's playground and The Round Pond for miniature boats. It is an ideal place for a leisurely stroll with a curious variety of statues to search out. There is the massive and powerful Physical Energy Statue, Speke's monument, the Elfin Oak carved with numerous fairies and goblins, Peter Pan with his fairy entourage and Henry Moore's leggy modern sculpture over the Long Water. The largest and most prominent statue is the Albert Memorial, with its pinnacle rising 173 feet, making a marvellous silhouette at dusk (covered at present due to restoration processes).

Facilities include: boating lake, bowling green, children's playgrounds, fishing (permit needed), putting, tennis courts.
Open: Hyde Park: *06.00-24.00 Mon-Sun;* Kensington Gardens: *07.00-½hr before dusk Mon-Sun.*
Free
Tube: Hyde Park Corner, High Street Kensington, Knightsbridge

Regent's Park and Primrose Hill NW1
071-486 7095

It is hard to believe now that this civilised area was once enclosed as a hunting park for Henry VIII. In 1811 it was redesigned for the Prince Regent, the chief architect being John Nash. He built the graceful terraces that line the edges and some of the mansions that are within the boundaries of the park.

In the area known as the Inner Circle is a magnificent rose garden, started in 1932 and dedicated to Queen Mary. The many other formal gardens are a riot of ever-changing colour, often with imaginative combinations of shades and shapes. There is also London Zoo (see page 58). You can walk along the canal to Little Venice and Paddington Basin to the west, and to the east, through Camden Lock, and the old railway lands of King's Cross to Islington Tunnel.

Primrose Hill, which is reached by crossing the canal and busy outer ring road, is indeed a veritable hill as anyone who does any running training hereabouts will testify. It is worth the slog to the top, however, as you get a wonderful panorama of London. There

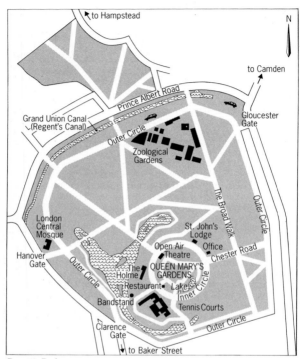

Regent's Park

is a helpful table to identify some of the most prominent tower blocks. As Primrose Hill remains open at night, with the paths well lit, it's a good place from which to see the lights of London.

Facilities include: boating lake, open-air theatre, tennis courts and facilities for football, baseball, rugby, cricket, a running track and London Zoo.

Open: Regent's Park: *05.00 (or dawn)-dusk Mon-Sun;* Primrose Hill: *24 hrs Mon-Sun.*
Free
Tube: Regent's Park, Baker Street, Chalk Farm   *BR:* Primrose Hill

Richmond Park, Surrey
081-948 3209
Richmond Park is the largest and least cultivated of the Royal parks. With little in the way of formal footpaths, there are acres of

open grass, bracken-covered slopes and pockets of woodland to explore.

It was Charles I who spotted the attraction of Richmond, which remains true today – far enough away from the city to get a bit of privacy and seclusion. He surrounded the area with a brick wall, much of which is still standing. There is a perimeter road, but come here for a genuine walk. A good way of getting to know the park is to walk the perimeter which, cutting the odd corner, is about seven miles. Once you've established your bearings you can start to criss cross the area and discover Pen Ponds and the gorgeous Isabella Plantation which is 42 acres of woodland garden in the south of the park. There is nothing formal here, just a mass of flowering shrubs, heather garden and a camellia walk watered by a stream.

Facilities include: children's playground, fishing (permit needed), flying field for model aeroplanes, golf courses.

Open: 07.00-½hr before dusk Mon-Sun.
Free
Tube/BR: Richmond

Richmond Park

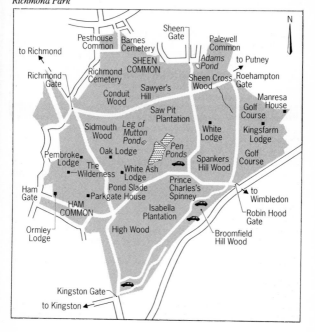

OUT AND ABOUT

THERE are plenty of possibilities for pleasant walking in and around London. A number of firms run themed tours on a fixed timetable. These are aimed principally at tourists and non-Londoners but are a fascinating and excellent way to get to know both new areas and famous buildings. Details of these organisations are listed below under 'Guided walks and tours'. Apart from these, most of the country parks and countryside centres run a programme of walks. Contact each individually to see what is on offer. There are also walks along London's canals (see section on Waterways page 70).

If you want to be independent, there are some self-guided walks in London which are listed in this section. These include historical areas, use of old railway tracks, canal towpaths and clever linking of open spaces such as the Green Chain Walk. Leaflets for these are available to help you find the route. In many of these there are circular walks or nature trails, or you can invent your own route by joining several adjacent parks. Alexandra Palace through Highgate and Queen's Woods and into Hampstead makes a substantial ramble in north London, or Dulwich Woods and Park, through the village to Brockwell Park is a good south London stroll.

Guided walks and tours

Citisights of London
213 Brooke Road, London E5 8AB
081-806 4325
Citisights run a huge variety of walking tours in London throughout the year. There is something to appeal to everyone with themes which include London's Criminal Underworld, John Betjeman's London, 200 Years along the City Wall and The Great Fire, Plague and Civil War. During the winter, the routes include more historical interiors, so there is a chance to shelter from the weather. Walks last around 2 hours.
Where to go: meet at a variety of venues, either the Museum of London or a tube station.
Times: There are *morning, afternoon* and *evening* walks.
Charge (accompanied children under 14 free)

City Walks of London
9-11 Kensington High Street, London W8 5HP
071-937 4281

Scare yourself silly with the late-night walk through London, *Ghosts, Ghouls and Haunted Taverns*; indulge in nostalgia by tracing the Rock routes of the Swinging Sixties or find out more about London's past on one of the many historical walks organised by this group. Subjects range from the original London of Dickens and Shakespeare to London of the Blitz. Walks last around 2 hours. No need to book, just turn up regardless of the weather.
Where to go: meeting places are usually at a tube station. Phone for details.
Times: Morning walks start from *10.30, afternoon* walks from *14.00, evening* walks from *19.00.*
Charge (accompanied children under 14 free)

Highgate Cemetery

Swain's Lane N6
081-340 1834
Highgate Cemetery lies astride Swain's Lane, and provides sights of Victorian values and semi-wild nature. The eastern part, which is where Karl Marx is buried, is open to the public. The western part, except for special occasions, is only accessible on a guided tour led by the Friends of Highgate Cemetery. Each guide has favourite anecdotes about the underground 'residents' and will lead the walk to different sections of the cemetery. Tours last about an hour and numbers are limited to about 25 (extra tours are laid on at busy times).
Where to go: all tours start at the cemetery.
Times: Apr-Oct 12.00, 14.00 & 16.00 Mon-Fri, between 11.00 & 16.00 Sat & Sun according to demand; Nov-Mar 12.00, 14.00 & 15.00 Mon-Fri; between 11.00 & 15.00 Sat & Sun according to demand.
Charge (children and Friends of Highgate Cemetery free)
Tube: Highgate

Historical Tours

3 Florence Road, South Croydon, Surrey CR2 0PQ
081-688 4019
These tours focus on London's history and cover a range of themes such as our legal heritage from Medieval times to the present and the working of the Old Bailey, to an exploration of London's Theatreland. There's a chance to visit many areas as diverse as the East End and Mayfair, Hampstead Heath and Docklands. Tours last about 2 hours. All you need to do is turn up, regardless of the weather.
Where to go: meeting places are usually at a tube station. Phone for details.
Times: Morning walks start at *11.00, afternoon* walks at *14.30, evening* walks from *19.00.*
Charge (accompanied children under 14 free)

Perfect London Walks
P.O. Box 1708, London NW6 1PQ
071-435 6413
This long-established walking tour group provide a varied selection of walks through the capital come rain or shine. *Discovering London* covers areas such as Bloomsbury, Soho, Mayfair and Highgate, and there are several pub walks through Belgravia, Hampstead and along the Thames. The pub walks take a little longer than the 2 hours you should allow for the others!
Where to go: meeting places are usually at a tube station. Phone for details.
Times: Morning walks start at *11.00, afternoon* walks at *14.00, evening* walks from *19.30*.
Charge (accompanied children under 16 free)

Tour Guides International
2 Bridge Street, London SW1A 2JR
071-839 2498/5314
Choose from three themed walks: *Government and Democracy, Royal London,* and *Upstairs Downstairs*. These are led by a Tourist Board Official Guide and run throughout the year whatever the weather.
Where to go: meet at The Tourist Information Centre, Victoria Station Forecourt SW1.
Times: Walks start at *14.30 Tue, Thur & Sat*.
Charge (accompanied children under 10 free)

Urban walks

The Green Chain Walk
The Green Chain Walk starts on the banks of the Thames and curves south for 16 miles through nearly 300 of south-east London's finest open spaces. The route passes through gardens, woods and commons including Woolwich Common, Maryon Park and Lesnes Abbey Woods with its ruined monastery. Amongst the many historic buildings along the way are Eltham Palace and Severndroog Castle (which is a fine viewing point). Four leaflets cover the whole of the route and are available from the Director of Leisure Services, Bromley Civic Centre, Rochester Avenue, Bromley BR1 3UH. 081-464 3333.

Epping Forest Centenary Walk
Epping Forest was saved from extinction by the City of London through an Act of Parliament passed in 1878. The 15-mile walk along the length of this beautiful forest was devised to celebrate the centenary in 1978. The route starts at Manor Park station and passes many of the best known places in the forest such as the Epping Forest Museum, and Connaught Water, the largest of the Forest's ponds. Epping Forest tracks can be notoriously muddy so do go well-prepared. If 15 miles all at once is a little daunting, there are good transport facilities along the way for anyone wanting to break the walk into smaller sections. There is a leaflet available for the Centenary Walk (small charge) from the Information

Officer, Epping Forest Conservation Centre, High Beach, Loughton, Essex. 081-508 7714.

The London Silver Jubilee Walkway

This 12-mile walkway was created for the Queen's Silver Jubilee in 1977. It circles the centre of London, passing close to many famous and historic buildings. The route starts at Leicester Square and is marked by 400 large discs (see diagram below) set in the pavement with smaller discs where there is a significant change of route. A leaflet is published by the Silver Jubilee Walkway Trust and is obtainable from the London Tourist Board, 26 Grosvenor Gardens SW1. 071-730 3488.

Diagrammatic plan of the Silver Jubilee Walkway

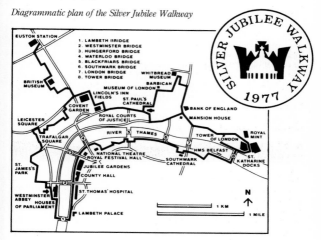

Parkland Walk

This 3¾ mile walk runs along the old railway line which used to connect Finsbury Park station with Alexandra Palace and was finally closed in 1970. Despite going through busy built-up areas, the high embankments shield you from the noise and bustle of London. The peacefulness has attracted many birds, and there are many different species of trees and flowers to see along the way.
Where to go: start at Finsbury Park. Access to the walk is from Oxford Road, Finsbury N4 or directly from the park. Finish at Muswell Hill.
Tube/BR: Finsbury Park

A walk through Spitalfields

Take a walk around the historic area of Spitalfields to appreciate its character and history. This part of London got its name from the hospital known as St Mary Spital and remained rural until the late 17th century. The first houses were built to accommodate silk weavers from France which started the area's close association with the clothing trade. In the 19th century, the clothing workshops were filled with Jewish refugees. In more recent times Bengalis have brought colour and flavour to the area. Apart from ethnic influences there are still many traces of Victorian and Georgian London. For details of the trail and a map send an sae to: The Tower Hamlets Environment Trust, 192-196 Hanbury Street, London E1 5HU. 071-377 0481.

Where to go: start at Liverpool Street station.

The Wandle Trail

This 12-mile trail was opened in 1988 and follows the River Wandle south from where it joins the Thames at Wandsworth to Beddington Park, Croydon. The walk takes you through parkland and industrial wasteland, urban street and garden suburb, a landscape far removed from earlier times when the river flowed through fields, osier plantations and watercress beds. For details of the trail contact the Wandle Industrial Museum, The Vestry Hall, London Road, Mitcham, Surrey. 081-648 0127 or the Ramblers' Association, 1-5 Wandsworth Road, London SW8 2XX. 071 582 6878.

Where to go: start in Wandsworth just north of Armoury Way SW18.
Tube: East Putney   *BR:* Putney or Wandsworth Town

Walking groups

Long Distance Walkers' Association

c/o The Secretary, Wayfarers, 9 Tainters Brook, Hempstead, Uckfield TN22 1UQ
(0825) 761803

This group has information on long-distance walks around the London area.

Ramblers' Association

1-5 Wandsworth Road, London SW8 2XX
071-582 6878

One of the best ways to enjoy walks through and around London is to join the Ramblers' Association. There are now four groups that cover the London area, organising regular local events as well as excursions further afield.

All rambles are led by experienced leaders who try to ensure no one gets lost or left behind. You don't need any special equipment, just stout shoes or boots, and be prepared for rain. If you want to take a dog, you must keep it on a lead. A lunch stop, and sometimes afternoon tea, is planned as part of the day.

Ramblers' Hotline

Phone 081-686 0636 for details of the current week's events organised by the London area of the Ramblers' Association.

WILDLIFE AND NATURAL HISTORY

LONDON contains a surprisingly rich variety of wildlife. Over 100 different types of bird breed in Greater London and there are some 2000 species of flora and fauna within 20 miles of St Paul's. Larger city-dwelling animals include foxes, badgers and deer. As the countryside has receded and many open spaces have disappeared, birds and animals have adapted and made use of Victorian cemeteries, abandoned railway lines and churchyards. Nevertheless, more care is needed to protect and enhance a variety of habitats to ensure that the richness of the city's wildlife is maintained. Both ancient and secondary woodland is important as is marshland, heath and meadowland. All these habitats can be found in Greater London and many are now protected by conservation and ecology groups.

Ecology centres

Capel Manor Environmental Centre
Bullsmoor Lane, Enfield, Middlesex EN1 4RQ
(0992) 24502
(0992) 763849 (courses office)
The centre is in the midst of a 65-acre estate comprising woodland, ponds, lakes and meadows. There are two nature trails, one for children and one for adults, and a natural history trail for finding out more about seasonal changes. There is an educational farm, which is open to the public on special days (phone for details) and a wardened campsite. In the centre itself are several displays on the environment.
Open: Farm: *Apr-Sep 13.00-18.00 Sat & Sun & school hols;* Gardens: *10.00-16.30 Mon-Fri.*
Charge
BR: Turkey Street

Epping Forest Conservation Centre
High Beach, Loughton, Essex
081-508 7714
Two nature trails start from the conservation centre going through a variety of habitats such as ancient beech woods, hedgerows and grassland, as well as the prehistoric earth works at Loughton Camp. The centre also runs a number of courses and study days on many aspects of the environment. Titles include *A Beginners*

Guide to Mosses, Know your Spiders and *The Birds of the North Kent Marshes*. There is also a programme of guided walks. For more information contact the Information Officer.
Open: Easter-end Oct 10.00-17.00 Wed-Sat, 11.00-17.00 Sun & Bank hols; Nov-Easter 10.00-17.00 Sat & Sun.
Free (small charge for guided walks)
Tube: Loughton   *BR:* Chingford

Sutton Ecology Centre
Old Rectory, Festival Walk, Carshalton, Surrey SM5 3NX
081-773 4018
Opened in 1989 by David Bellamy, the four acres surrounding the centre include a variety of natural habitats such as marsh and grassland, pond and woodland. Each habitat is well signposted so that you can identify at a glance some of the flora and fauna that might be around. The centre encourages learning about the work needed to manage each habitat.

The Borough of Sutton has a committment to recycling and at the ecology centre there are facilities to recycle bottles, paper, rags and tins. There are also displays on alternative technology using solar and wind power, as well as exhibition gardens showing urban dwellers ideas of what they can achieve at home.

The centre runs courses for schools and holiday play schemes. Activities include anything from pond dipping to making musical instruments out of scrap materials.

The centre is also the meeting place for the Sutton Conservation Group, so if you want to get involved locally, contact them or Bruce Cockrean, the Community Ecologist at the above address.
Open: 10.00-16.00 Mon-Sat.
Free
BR: Carshalton

Ecology groups

London Ecology Unit
Bedford House, 125 Camden High Street, London NW1 7JR
071-267 7944
The London Ecology Unit advises boroughs on ecology and conservation work, producing detailed ecology handbooks which list sites, types of habitat and so on. They also produce a complete gazetteer of the hundreds of nature reserves in the Greater London Area, as well as a book on how to set up and run a nature reserve or ecological area.
Tube: Camden Town

London Natural History Society
P.C. Holland (Membership Secretary), Flat 9, Pinewood Court, Clapham, London SW4 8LB
The London Natural History Society was founded in 1858. Its aims are to promote the awareness and understanding of our environ-

ment on which successful conservation depends. The Society has a tremendous knowledge of the ever-changing wildlife and vegetation of London such as how many species of bird have been recorded here, or how many moths and butterflies.

There are plenty of field meetings in the London area, generally at weekends. These are informal with experienced leaders to guide beginners. You might find yourself studying the ecology and entomology of Hampstead Heath, or ornithology at Staines Reservoir.

London Wildlife Trust
80 York Way, London N1 9AG
071-278 6612

The aims of the London Wildlife Trust are to protect open space in London, and to make the public aware of the variety of wildlife that exists in the city.

When the Trust manage an open space, they try and create suitable habitats for a variety of plants and animals, both land-based and aquatic. They now manage some 60 sites across London, and have seven where there are staff on hand who can show you round and answer questions. These are listed in the section on Nature reserves (see page 48).

The Trust was founded in 1981 by a group of volunteers, but now employs over 30 staff. They welcome help either for odd days or at weekends. Jobs include tree planting, path maintenance and pond clearance. If you are really keen, you can join 'The Newt Squad', a group organised by the central office, who have work on nearly every weekend. The London Wildlife Trust supplies the tools and the training, all you need are old clothes and wellies. Volunteers come in all shapes and sizes and a mixture of age groups, but if you're aged 12 or under you could join 'Watch' which is especially for youngsters. There are a number of 'Watch' groups that are active in London, and the Trust can give you the address of your local branch.
Tube: King's Cross St Pancras

Trust for Urban Ecology
Stave Hill Nature Park, Timber Pond Road, Rotherhithe, London SE16 1AG
071-237 9165

This trust (originally The Ecology Park Trust) was set up in 1977. They specialise in the creation of natural habitats in the urban environment and advising land-owners on how derelict sites and wasteland can be redesigned to attract wildlife. They conduct habitat surveys, teach ecology and run wide-ranging educational courses.

The Trust manages three nature reserves in the south of London: Dulwich Upper Wood Nature Park, Lavender Pond, and Stave Hill, where their office is based. Open days are held at all these sites when there are guided walks, displays on natural history and a chance to learn about food from the wild. They also

welcome volunteers who can turn up on a daily basis and help with tree planting, path construction or building bird boxes. Telephone the office to find out on which days they need help.
Tube: Rotherhithe

Nature reserves

Where no opening times are given in the following section, access is given during daylight hours. It is advisable, however, to **phone and check in advance.**

Camley Street Natural Park
12 Camley Street NW1
071-833 2311
This two-acre site, managed by the London Wildlife Trust, is a haven for a variety of wildlife in the midst of the busy back streets and railway lines of King's Cross and St Pancras. The word 'natural' is somewhat misleading as the park has been entirely created from wasteland during the last six years. It is now well established with flourishing tree life, a thriving pond, reed beds and meadows all bordered on one side by the peaceful Regent's Canal. It's a delight to hear the noise of birds and wildfowl over the traffic as well as see butterflies, frogs and toads and the rich variety of plant life.
Open: 09.00-17.00 Mon-Fri, 11.00-17.00 Sat & Sun.
Free
Tube: King's Cross

Crane Park Island
Twickenham, Middlesex
(Access from Ellerman Avenue or Hanworth Road)
081-898 9582
Managed by the London Wildlife Trust, this interesting site is an island in the River Crane. Habitats include reed beds and meadowland as well as some mature woodland, contrasting well with the more traditional park near by. Large numbers of woodland birds nest here including blackcap and spotted fly catchers. The water in the river is comparatively free from pollution and as a result a wide range of water animals are to be found including fresh-water shrimps, three-spined sticklebacks and marsh frogs.
Free
Tube/BR: Richmond *BR:* Hounslow East, Whitton

Dulwich Upper Park Wood
c/o Bowley Close Centre, Farquhar Road, Crystal Palace SE19
081-761 6230
This 5½ acre site (not to be confused with Dulwich Woods) consists of a patch of ancient woodland and the neglected gardens of Victorian houses that were bombed in the war and vacated in the 1960s. The vegetation has now reverted to secondary woodland. There are over 200 species of plant and 230 different types of fungi

as well as many invertebrates. Some exotic plants from the original gardens still survive.
Free
BR: Gypsy Hill

Gillespie Park
Gillespie Road, Highbury N5
071-354 5413
Here's a chance for green horizons in one of London's heavily built-up areas. This small natural park has an interesting mixture of habitats within its three acres. There are meadows with typical wasteland flowers and grasses, scrubland of elderberry and dog rose, new mixed woodland of oak, birch and pine as well as Islington's only pond.

Once in the park, the air seems cleaner and fresher, and there is a surprising sense of space. Ideal for a breath of countryside in the midst of city life. There are on-site wardens to give information and care for the place.
Free
Tube: Arsenal

Gunnersbury Triangle

Bollo Lane, Chiswick W4
081-747 3881
This triangle of open land was once surrounded by three busy railway lines. During the Second World War, the area was converted into allotments to produce much needed food for the war effort. Since then the site has regenerated secondary woodland with plenty of silver birch and also pond and wet flush. The site is managed by the London Wildlife Trust. Regular open days are held here as well as practical work days (often on a Sunday).
Free
Tube: Chiswick Park

Lavender Pond Nature Park

Lavender Road, off Rotherhithe Street SE16
071-232 0498
This is the place to come if you are interested in aquatic wildlife and its habitat. As the name suggests, there is a pond here as well as reed beds, alder carr and some mixed woodland. The site is popular with schools and those wishing to visit should contact the teacher at the Pump House, an old pumping station on site (071-231 2976).
Open: Access is restricted when the swing bridge is in use.
Free
Tube: Surrey Docks, Rotherhithe

London Wildlife Garden & Nursery

28 Marsden Road, Peckham SE5
071-252 9186
This small site used to be a council depot but is now an innovative venture for the London Wildlife Trust. Over the last two years they have created a number of demonstration habitats here such as a back garden plot and a pond to show different ways of creating areas suitable for wildlife. They also grow wild flowers and trees to stock their own sites throughout London, though a limited number are on sale.
Open: 09.30-17.00 Mon-Thur, 14.00-dusk Sun. (These times may be extended during summer months, phone for details).
Free
BR: East Dulwich

St Mary Magdalen Churchyard

Nature Reserve and Interpretative Centre, Norman Road, East Ham E6
081-470 4525
This nature reserve is in Britain's largest churchyard, 10 acres with St Mary's in the centre still regularly used. A hedge, planted round the medieval boundary, divides the neat and tidy section needed for wedding photos from the rest of the site which is going wild in a controlled way. There are several different habitats,

mixed woodland and open grassy areas, plus a picnic space if you've gone for a whole day out.

The Interpretative Centre is mainly used by schools but there is a small display section and shop on the ground floor.

Open: Nature Reserve: *Mar-Oct 09.00-17.00 Mon-Sun; Nov-Feb 09.00-dusk Mon-Sun;* Interpretative Centre: *14.00-17.00 Tue, Thur, Sat & Sun.*
Free
Tube: East Ham (then by bus 101)

Sydenham Hill Wood
Sydenham Hill SE26
081-699 5698/071-278 6612
Sydenham Hill Wood is one of the last surviving fragments of the Great North Wood which once covered much of south London. The oaks and hornbeams are direct descendants of trees which were established after the last Ice Age, 10,000 years ago. The woodland attracts 60 types of breeding birds including woodpeckers and owls, as well as some species not normally associated with cities such as the nuthatch and tree creeper. The London Wildlife Trust, who manage 30 acres, have installed a pond to provide variety. There are practical work days held here as well as guided tours.
Free
BR: Sydenham Hill

Tump 53
Harrow Manor Way, Abbey Wood SE2
Sounding more like something out of a Sci-fi novel than a nature reserve, this site was originally an ammunition dump and part of the extensive Woolwich Arsenal. Moated ammunition stores or 'Tumps' were built in the nineteenth century, but they became run down after the First World War and were left virtually untouched until management by the London Wildlife Trust in the mid-eighties. The site now consists of a large area of water with reed beds, meadowland and woodland. There are nesting sites for water fowl and the moat is home to frogs, toads and newts. On the nearby Thames, there are different varieties of wading birds.
Free
BR: Abbey Wood

Walthamstow Marsh Nature Reserve
(0992) 893345
Walthamstow Marsh has been designated an SSSI as it is one of the last examples of semi-natural wetland in Greater London. The area contains a number of plants typical of former flood meadows such as sedge marsh and reed swamp. The hay meadows with their traditional flowers are also interesting. Butterflies such as the Essex Skipper and many breeding birds are attracted. There are interpretation panels on the site giving a brief introduction and orientation to the wildlife and history.

Just nearby is the Middlesex Filter Beds Nature Reserve The filter beds were constructed in the mid-19th century to clean the water following a cholera epidemic. Varying thicknesses of sand and gravel were left in the beds on closure and over the years each bed has been colonised by a rich mixture of aquatic, marsh and woodland wildlife.
Free
BR: Clapton, Walthamstow Central

The Welsh Harp (Brent Reservoir)
Birchen Grove NW9
081-900 5016/206 0492
The 170 acres of The Welsh Harp, as it is commonly known, is an important nature reserve as well as a centre for many watersports activities. Designated an SSSI, the reservoir and its shores, with their rich mixture of wetland and waterside habitats, attract a huge number of breeding birds, through spring, summer and winter. Some 140 species can be seen here including one of Britain's biggest colonies of great-crested grebe. There are specially-designed nesting rafts which are popular with the common tern and many waterfowl. Plant and insect life is also varied and there is a special artificial bat hibernaculum (bat cave!) Contact the Countryside Ranger for information about guided walks, local conservation groups and the bat cave on the above number.
Tube: Wembley Park, Neasden

Nature trails

There are many nature trails through London's open spaces. Most Country Parks have at least one trail and often a leaflet to help you identify particular features along the way. The majority of the nature reserves detailed above have trails to guide you round and many local boroughs have developed nature trails. Contact your local leisure services to see what is available in your area. They can also put you in touch with local conservation groups. It may be best to join specific walks for bird- or bat-watching for example. These are on offer at country parks or by joining the London Natural History Society (see page 47). For further information on London's nature trails contact the London Tourist Board, 26 Grosvenor Gardens SW1. 071-730 3488.

City farms

It wasn't so long ago that farm animals were commonplace in London. Pigs and chickens were kept in backyards and cows grazed on common land. Stricter rules on health and housing changed this and the animals got moved out into the countryside. In the last fifteen years the situation has been very slightly reversed with the development of City farms, some twenty of which have sprung up all over London. Many are community-run, making use of wasteland areas which would otherwise be derelict. Activities, animals, and facilities vary from one place to another giving each farm its own character. Some farms welcome volunteers to help with general maintenance, feeding animals and looking after visitors, and many provide schemes and clubs for children to learn about life on the farm. In most cases there is no admission charge.

Several of the farms have cafés and shops selling an interesting range of produce from organic vegetables to dairy foods, eggs, meat and herbs, plus plenty of manure!

College Farm
Fitzalan Road, Finchley N3
081-349 0690
Rare-breed cattle and Shire horses are amongst the animals here. On the first Sunday of every month (except January) there is a country fair including donkey rides, craft demonstrations and a market.
Open: 10.00-18.00 Mon-Sun (except 13.00-18.00 first Sunday of the month).
Charge
Tube: Finchley Central

Corams Fields
93 Guildford Street WC1
071-837 6138
This farm is run in conjunction with a large children's playground. There are plenty of smaller animals to see including a tortoise, as well as aviaries with budgies and canaries. Other facilities include a large adventure playground, lawns and a paddling pool. It's a good place to spend the day but note – no adults unless accompanied by children!
Open: Mar-Oct 09.00-20.00 Mon-Sun; Nov-Feb 09.00-17.00 Mon-Sun.
Free
Tube: Russell Square

Deen City Farm
1 Batsworth Road, Mitcham, Surrey
081-648 1461
Animals here range in size from rabbits to cows. There is also an

organic horticultural area and allotments. Produce grown is either sold or used in the on-site vegetarian café. The riding school has facilities for the disabled, offers pony rides, jumping and hacking classes as well as Voltige – acrobatics on horse back for aspiring circus performers.
Open: 09.00-16.00 (riding school until 20.00) Tue-Sun.
Free (charge for riding school)
Tube: Colliers Wood

Elm Farm
Gladstone Terrace, Lockington Road, Battersea SW8
071-627 1130
Young (very young!) farmers can start off here helping with the sheep, goats, poultry and cattle on a Saturday when this farm runs its special children's club. Other facilities include a café which serves hot meals every day (except Sunday) and has goat's and sheep's milk on sale as well as seasonal vegetables and herbs.
Open: 09.30-16.00 Tue-Sun (closed Fri).
Free
BR: Battersea Park

Freightliners Farm
Paradise Park, Sheringham Road, Holloway N7
071-609 0467
There is a complete range of farm animals kept here and visitors are welcome to help. This farm also takes on volunteers on a more regular basis giving them training in all aspects of livestock management. There is also complete disabled access to the farm and all its buildings.
Open: 09.30-13.00 & 14.00-16.30 Tue-Sun.
Free
Tube: Holloway Road, Caledonian Road

Hackney City Farm
1A Goldsmiths Row E2
071-729 6381
The farm buildings were converted from a brewery whilst the surrounding two acres have been gradually brought into productive use. The range of animals includes Southdown sheep who are bred for fine quality wool. There are also honey-producing hives, an ecological pond and wildlife area plus a herb knot-garden to enjoy. Volunteers are always welcome. Help is needed at feeding times, for planting work and general maintenance. From the farm there is an urban park and farm trail which takes in nearby Haggerston Park.
Open: 10.00-16.40 Tue-Sun.
Free
Tube: Bethnal Green

Hayes Hill and Holyfieldhall Farms
Stubbins Hall Lane, Crooked Mill, Waltham Abbey, Essex
(099289) 2291 (Mon-Fri) (099289) 2781 (Sat & Sun)
Whatever the time of year there is always something to see: new-
born animals in spring, sheep shearing in the summer and harvest-
ing in the autumn. It is also possible to watch the daily milking
routine and on Sundays in summer there are demonstrations of a
range of rural crafts such as spinning and weaving. In the 16thC
barn there's a display of farm implements.
Open: 10.00-16.30 Mon-Fri, 10.00-18.00 Sat & Sun.
Charge
BR: Waltham Cross (then by bus 253 from Waltham Abbey)

Kentish Town City Farm
1 Cressfield Close NW5
071-482 2861
Children and adults can have a perfect introduction to farm animals here as the livestock are very visitor-friendly. There are some
rare-breed pigs and sheep as well as Belted-Galloway cattle.
Feeding times are at *09.30 & 16.00 daily.* On Sundays at *13.30*
there are pony rides. In the summer, the farm runs holiday play
schemes for children (age 7-16) who want to experience daily life
on the farm.
Open: 09.00-18.00 Mon-Sun.
Free
Tube: Kentish Town, Chalk Farm *BR:* Gospel Oak

Mudchute Farm
Pier Street, Millwall E14
071-515 5901
When Millwall Docks were built towards the end of the 19th cent-
ury, the mud excavated was dumped on this site – hence the name
'Mudshute'. In an attractive setting just across from Greenwich
Park, this 32-acre farm is the largest of the inner city farms. An
education worker is on hand who can help explain and demon-
strate many aspects of farming. Apart from all the usual animals
there are some more exotic species such as llamas and Vietnamese
Pot Bellied pigs. There is also a riding stable on the premises (open
Wed- Sun) for which there is a *charge*.
Open: 09.00-17.00 Mon-Sun.
Free
DLR: Island Gardens

Newham City Farm
King George Avenue, Plaistow E16
071-476 1170
This farm has an ever-changing selection of farm animals as well
as the more unusual llamas and wallabies. You can ride in a cart
pulled by a magnificent shire horse, have light refreshments in the

farm's café, and buy produce (as available) such as goat's milk and free-range eggs.
Open: 10.00-17.45 Mon-Sun.
Free
Tube: Plaistow

Spitalfields Farm Association
Weaver Street E1
071-247 8762
Spitalfields Farm is an oasis of green in a very congested part of London. It has been running for over 10 years on former wasteland and an area leased from British Rail. Apart from the animals, regular features include craftwork, bee-keeping, courses for adults in food and farming or herbalism and holiday play schemes for children. To find out more about the fascinating area of Spitalfields, try one of the farm's historical horse and cart tours. Sample farm produce at their café.
Open: 09.00-18.00 Mon-Sun.
Free
Tube: Shoreditch (rush hour only), Whitechapel, Bethnal Green, Aldgate East

Stepping Stones Farm
Corner of Stepney Way & Stepney High Street E1
071-790 8204
In the middle of the East End and set up to make use of inner city land which would otherwise be derelict, this is a community-based project with local people volunteering to help out and keep it running. Everyone is welcome to visit and lend a hand. Livestock can change according to the seasons but usually includes pigs, goats, cows, sheep, ducks, geese, rabbits and a donkey. There's a strong educational bias with tours round the farm and an introduction to the animals and their roles. Projects show you how wool is spun, milk is made into cheese and crops grown from seed to produce grain.
Open: 09.30-18.00 Tue-Sun.
Free
Tube: Stepney Green   *Docklands Light Railway:* Stepney East

Surrey Docks Farm
Rotherhithe Street SE16
071-231 1010
This two-acre farm is in a most attractive setting opposite Canary Wharf on the banks of the Thames. A good range of farm animals are kept here with some rare breed chickens and beehives. They have teaching facilities for adults with special needs and educational facilities for schools.
Open: 10.00-13.00 & 14.00-17.00 Tue-Sun.
Free
Tube: Surrey Docks, Rotherhithe

Vauxhall City Farm
24 St Oswald's Place, Lambeth SE11
071-582 4204
Donkey and horse rides, and a small wildlife pond, are part of the facilities here. Animals kept include goats, sheep, rabbits and ferrets as well as cattle. There are group tours organised during the week to explain about the animals and how the farm works. Volunteers are welcome to help with any of the chores. On Saturdays from *11.30* a group of experienced spinners demonstrate the craft and will give advice to beginners.
Open: 10.30-17.00 Tue-Thur, Sat & Sun.
Free
Tube: Vauxhall

Walworth City Farm
230 Amelia Street SE17
071-582 2652
This is a not strictly-speaking a farm as the only 'animals' kept are bees! It is a horticultural centre with a solar dome and poly-tunnel and is a good place to go to see organic and energy saving methods of gardening in action. They grow a range of exotic Afro-Caribbean plants and vegetables, as well as many medicinal and culinary herbs, and historical plants such as Victorian cottage garden flowers. Limited seasonal produce is on sale.
Open: 10.00-17.00 Mon-Sat.
Free
Tube: Kennington

Wellgate Community Farm
Collier Row Road, Romford, Essex
081-599 0415
This small farm has plenty to offer, all scaled down to match the size of the place. They keep all the usual farm animals except cattle for which there is insufficient space. Volunteers are welcome, and they have a holiday scheme for children.
Open: 09.00-16.00 Mon-Fri, 09.00-12.00 Sat & Sun.
Free
BR: Romford (then by bus 247)

Zoos and animal enclosures

Chessington World of Adventures
Leatherhead Road, Chessington, Surrey
(0372) 727227
Not just a zoo any longer, Chessington now also houses a spectacular family fair with rides such as the Mystic East, Calamity Canyon and the Vampire – a hanging roller coaster. The zoo comprises 65 acres and includes a bird garden, children's zoo and polar bear plunge. If you want to take a group to the zoo contact (0372) 729560 to book.

Open: mid Mar-Oct 10.00-17.00 Mon-Sun; Nov-mid Mar (zoo only)
10.00-16.00 Mon-Sun.
Charge
BR: Chessington South

London Zoo
Regent's Park NW1
071-722 3333
The Zoological gardens, opened in 1828, were laid out by Decimus
Burton. The original collection of animals included monkeys,
bears, llamas and zebras. From the start, the zoo was a major
attraction. Early visitors were reprimanded for poking parasols
through the bars! Since 1959 the buildings and gardens have been
redesigned to include a new aviary and lion terrace that are far
removed from the restrictive original cages. If you are a keen sup-
porter of London Zoo, it is possible to become a zoo volunteer.
After free training, you can guide visiting groups, help keep the
zoo tidy and be on hand at the information centres. For more
details contact the Zoo Volunteer Co-ordinator at the above address.
*Open: Apr-Sep 09.00-18.00 Mon-Sun; Oct-Mar 10.00-16.00 Mon-
Sun.*
Charge
Tube: Regent's Park, Great Portland Street, Camden Town

Whipsnade Animal Park
Dunstable, Bedfordshire
(0582) 872171
A 500-acre 'natural' zoo of woods and downland in the Chilterns.
There are over 2000 animals in large open-air enclosures and some
species roam freely throughout the park. You can picnic in the
grounds, so take binoculars or use the telescopes provided. You
can travel within the park in you own car or by the miniature
motor-coach train. There is also a children's adventure playground.
*Open: 10.00-dusk (or 18.00) Mon-Fri, 10.00-dusk (or 19.00) Sat &
Sun.*
Charge
BR: Luton (then by bus 43)

Windsor Safari Park
Winkfield Road, Windsor, Berkshire
(0753) 869841
Drive round the park in the car, for which there are long queues in
summer, with windows closed, to see the many wild animals
including white rhinos. Alternatively there are walks through the
tropical plant and butterfly house, chimpanzee enclosure and
Noah's Ark adventure centre as well as dolphin, sealion and parrot
shows.
Open: 10.00-dusk Mon-Sun.
Charge
BR: Windsor (or by car)

Woburn Wild Animal Kingdom & Leisure Park
Woburn, Bedfordshire
(0525) 290407
The largest drive-through safari park in Britain. Rare European bison, wallabies, llamas, rheas and other animals roam freely, sometimes very near, so keep the windows closed! There are also sea-lions, parrot shows and elephant displays and a leisure area with rides, boating lakes and a cable car. The 3000-acre leisure park, which is separate from the Animal Kingdom, contains the original herd of Pere David deer, saved from extinction by the 11th Duke of Bedford.
Open: mid Mar-end Oct 10.00-17.00 Mon-Sun.
Charge
Access by car only

Apart from the zoos, there are opportunities to see a variety of animals on the City farms (see page 53), or at some of the small animal and bird enclosures in the following parks:

Battersea Park SW11
Small zoo with sheep and pygmy goats as well as wallabies, deer, monkeys and parrots.

Clissold Park N16
Two ornamental lakes attract a variety of bird life. There are also deer and a miniature zoo, as well as an aviary.

Crystal Palace Park N16
Small zoo with some tame animals for children to pat as well as a variety of caged birds.

Golders Hill Park NW11
There are colourful flamingoes on the small lake as well as caged birds and a number of deer, wallabies and goats.

Greenwich Park SE10
About 30 deer are kept in the enclosure here and have been a feature of the park since the 16th century.

Holland Park W8
Noisy peacocks are the main bird in the woodlands here. There are also a number of ducks and rabbits and very tame squirrels.

Horniman Gardens SE23
There is a small children's zoo here as well as a number of caged birds.

Victoria Park E2
There is a small deer pen in the park, also with rabbits and guinea pigs.

Archaeology and conservation

London, ever-spreading and in constant development, needs protection as much as Britain's most famous beauty spots, to preserve the heritage of the past whilst meeting the needs of the present and future. The past is an important part of the city, and most Londoners have a sense of it. For anyone wishing to be more involved, there are several groups concerned with archaeology which are listed here. There are also plenty of opportunities for getting involved in improving the present-day environment, conservation work and preserving green spaces.

Archaeology

There is a wide variety of work and projects available on discovering and preserving the archaeology of London. Contact the Museum of London, 150 London Wall, London EC2Y 5HN. 071-600 3699 for details. Most of the projects require some commitment in terms of time.

Conservation work

British Trust for Conservation Volunteers
80 York Way N1
071-278 4293
The British Trust for Conservation Volunteers gives everyone the chance to do something practical for the environment. They run a whole range of projects from pond and stream-clearing to restoring footpaths and creating inner-city nature reserves. Whether you want to give one day or several, or if you are only free mid-week or weekends, there will be something for you to get involved in. Most of the one-day tasks take place in the Greater London Area, whilst mid-week residential schemes venture further afield from deepest Berkshire to the Isle of Wight. All projects are suitable for first time volunteers.

To find out more, get in touch with them at their London office, or turn up to a volunteers evening. These are informal occasions held on the third Wednesday of every month where you can see a slide show of BTCV's work and chat to the staff. The meetings are held at the York Way office and start at *18.30*. If you can't easily get to central London and prefer to be involved in conservation work nearer home, contact BTCV for their list of over 40 local groups throughout the London area.

Colne Valley Park Groundwork Trust
Denham Court Mansion, Village Road, Denham, Uxbridge, Middlesex UB9 5BG
(0895) 832662

This independent Charitable Trust was set up to tackle problems with the neglected and degraded landscape throughout the Colne Valley on the western edge of London. Volunteers are welcomed every Sunday from *09.30-17.00* to help with a variety of projects from scrub and ragwort removal to pond clearance and fence building. Pick up point is Uxbridge Tube station. It is advisable to wear old clothes and bring a packed lunch. The programme of Sunday tasks is printed in their volunteer news. Phone for more details.

National Trust
The Volunteer Unit, PO Box 12, Westbury, Wiltshire BA13 4NA (0373) 826826

There's more to helping the National Trust look after their properties than a spot of rhodo-bashing. The wide variety of jobs suitable for volunteers includes room stewarding and outdoor work such as surveying. They are always on the look out for those with useful professional skills.

There are comparatively few National Trust properties in Greater London, but to help at these or elsewhere in the Home Counties contact your nearest Regional Volunteer Co-ordinator.

Southern region: John Sursham, Polesden Lacey, Dorking, Surrey RH5 6BD. (0372) 53401.

Thames & Chilterns region: Jenny Baker, Hughenden Manor, High Wycombe, Bucks HP14 4LA. (0494) 28051.

East Anglia region (includes east London): Peter Giles, Blickling, Norwich NR11 6NF. (0263) 733471.

Kent & East Sussex region (includes south-east London): David Soesan, Estate Office, Scotney, Lamberhurst, Tunbridge Wells, Kent TN3 8JN. (0892) 890651

CALENDAR OF OUTDOOR EVENTS

Spring (March/April/May)

MARCH

Easter Day Parade
Battersea Park SW11
081-871 6363
Taking place on Easter Sunday (which could be in March or April, depending on the year) in the park, there is entertainment including jugglers, stilt walkers and a jazz tent from midday. The parade starts at *15.00* and includes floats, marching bands and all sorts of carnival elements with music from the Caribbean, Latin-America, and American majorettes. To enter a float, phone the special events department of Wandsworth Council: 081-871 6000 and they will send you the appropriate form.
Free
BR: Battersea Park

APRIL

London Harness Horse Parade
Regent's Park NW1
071-486 7905
This parade of 200 working horses takes place on Easter Monday. Many different breeds are on show from the heavy Shire horses and Somerset breeds to lighter-weight animals used for pulling bakers' vans. Judging takes place in the Inner Circle about *09.30* and there is a parade around the Outer Circle at *midday*.
Free
Tube: Regent's Park, Baker Street, Great Portland Street

London Marathon
081-948 7935
With some 25,000 starters, this has become the world's largest road race. International runners lead the crowd, and behind come a mixture of serious runners, joggers, celebrities and fancy dress fun runners. There is a marvellous atmosphere for both competitors and spectators alike. One of the best spots to watch is at Greenwich, where it all starts, then use the foot tunnel to catch up with the runners or go straight to the finish at Westminster Bridge! If you wish to take part contact the above telephone number.
Free for spectators, charge for competitors
DLR: Island Gardens (then via foot tunnel)   *BR:* Greenwich

Oxford v. Cambridge Boat Race
071-730 3488

The annual battle between the light and the dark blues has been going on since 1845. There are plenty of vantage points such as bridges and riverside pubs. The start is at Putney and the finish up-river at Mortlake.

Tube: Putney Bridge (start)   *BR:* Mortlake (finish)

MAY

Chelsea Flower Show
Chelsea Royal Hospital, Royal Hospital Road SW3

071-834 4333 or 071-828 1744 (24hr recorded information)

The grounds of the Royal Hospital Chelsea burst into bloom during the third week of May. Over 4 days, 11 acres are given over to a mass of exhibitors showing specially designed gardens, fruit and vegetable displays, garden equipment and everything horticultural. Postal applications for tickets to: Chelsea Flower Show Ticket Office, P.O. Box 407, London SE11 5ET. Credit Card Hotline: 071-735 6199.

Charge

Tube: Sloane Square

Glyndebourne Festival Opera Season
Glyndebourne, nr Lewes, East Sussex.

(0273) 541111

A traditional outing for Londoners who flock to hear superlative singing and dine out on the lawn. The concerts take place throughout the summer from May to August.

Open Air Art Exhibitions
There are several places in London where you can view (and buy!) a wide variety of paintings unencumbered by roofs, walls and neon lighting.

Victoria Embankment Gardens WC2 - artists and their work are on display in the first two weeks of May and from Monday to Saturday during August.

The Terrace, Richmond Hill, Richmond, Surrey. Run by the Richmond Art Group, there are exhibitions in May or June from *10.00-20.00* Saturday and Sunday.

Royal Avenue, King's Road SW3. Exhibitions from May-October from *11.00-18.00* on Saturday.

All year round artists exhibit their work every Sunday morning against the railings on the Green Park side of Piccadilly and along Bayswater Road outside Kensington Gardens and Hyde Park.

Free

Victoria Embankment Gardens: *Tube:* Embankment

The Terrace: *Tube/BR*: Richmond

Royal Avenue: *Tube:* Sloane Square

Summer (June/July/August)

JUNE

Annual London International Festival of Street Entertainers

071-287 0907 (Alternative Arts)

This competition takes place in Golden Square, Soho W1 and the pedestrianised areas around Carnaby Street W1. There's plenty to see with acts changing roughly every 20 minutes on each of the 15 or so pitches. They start mid-morning and go through to early evening. There's plenty of variety too, with categories such as juggling, clowning, dance, theatre and mime. The competition moves into a theatre on the final evening.

Free in the street, charge in the theatre

Tube: Piccadiilly Circus, Oxford Circus

Cadbury's London Strollathon

Freepost, One Small Step Appeal, London SE16 4BR

Hotline 071-232 2255

Started in 1990, this 10-mile walk through London aims to raise money for charitable projects. Top of the list is a movement laboratory for children with cerebral palsy. The walk, starting in the morning, is open to everyone, including those with disabilites. The route in 1991 starts in Hyde Park, near Lancaster Gate tube, and winds round Little Venice, the West End, City and St Katherine's Dock finishing on the South Bank.

Derby Day

Epsom Race Course, Epsom, Surrey

(0372) 726311

This world famous race was started in 1780 and now runs on the first Wednesday in June on the airy course high up on the North Downs. To see the race, just turn up on the day for tickets. The most expensive places in the grandstand give a good view of the race, whilst entry to the Paddock means you can only watch the horses parade. Apart from the race, other entertainments include a huge fair, market and numerous fortune tellers! Can they tell you where to place your bets?

Charge

BR: Tattenham Corner (from Victoria or London Bridge)

Greenwich Festival

081-317 8687

All sorts of outdoor activities and events take place in Greenwich in June. There are walks, talks, folk and classical music shows and a variety of entertainments for children and adults from Punch & Judy to outdoor concerts. The dates vary each year so phone the above number for exact details.

Free and charge (depending on event)

BR: Greenwich

Hampton Court Palace International Flower Show

Hampton Court Palace, Hampton Court, Surrey

081-977 0050

This show started in 1990 and is held in the delightful park behind Hampton Court. The 20 acres are filled with all manner of flowers and flower arrangements, plants and gardening accessories from furniture to fountains. The show is in mid-June, and lasts for five days, from *10.00* to *early evening* with plants sold on the last afternoon.

Charge

Tube: Hammersmith (then by bus 267) *BR:* Hampton Court

Henley Royal Regatta

Henley-on-Thames, Oxfordshire

(0491) 572153

A traditional annual event, where rowing and socialising take place side by side. Smart outfits and even smarter picnics try to outdo each other whilst watching the skilled rowers do their stuff. For further information on how to enter a race or their exact dates, phone the above number.

BR: Henley-on-Thames

London to Brighton Bike Ride

Bike Events, P.O. Box 75, Bath, Avon

(0225) 310859

This is the most famous of the long-distance bike rides from the capital. It starts on Clapham Common from *05.30* in the morning until about *10.30*. Write for an entry form to Bike Events and also for details of other London bike rides such as London to Oxford or London to Southend.

Free for spectators, charge for riders

Royal Ascot Race Meeting

Ascot Racecourse, Ascot, Berks

(0344) 22211

A famously smart event with a chance to see hats, horses and royalty during three days of racing. Takes place from Tuesday to Friday but the exact dates vary from year to year. Phone for details.

Charge

BR: Ascot

Trooping the Colour

Horse Guards Parade SW1

071-930 4466

This colourful ceremony, usually held on the second Saturday in June, marks the occasion of the Queen's Official Birthday. The royal party leaves Buckingham Palace shortly after *10.30*, but you need to get there much earlier to get a place along the Mall. There is a ballot for tickets; to enter, write by the end of February to: The Brigade Major (Trooping the Colour), Household Division, Horse

Guard's Parade SW1 enclosing an sae. There is a maximum of two tickets per application.
Charge
Tube: St James's Park, Charing Cross

Wimbledon Lawn Tennis Championships
All England Lawn Tennis & Croquet Club, P.O. Box 98, Church Road, Wimbledon SW19
081-946 2244 (recorded information)
One of the most famous championships in the world. It takes place during the last week of June and the first week of July and attracts huge crowds. Seats for Centre and No. 1 courts are allocated by public ballot (one application form per address), but you can queue for tickets for the other courts on the day of play. Strawberries and cream (though rather expensive!) are the traditional accompaniment.
Tube: Southfields   *BR/Tube:* Wimbledon (then by special bus)

JULY

Doggett's Coat & Badge Race
071-626 3531
This race was started in 1715 to commemorate the accession of George I and has been run every year since. Limited to six watermen newly out of apprenticeship, they race in single sculls from London Bridge to Chelsea Bridge. The prize is scarlet livery and a silver badge. Phone for details of exact time and day of race.
BR/Tube: London Bridge

Swan Upping
Ownership of the swans on the Thames is divided between the Dyers Company, the Vintners Company and the Sovereign. Each year a census of the swans on the reaches up to Henley is taken, and the cygnets are branded by nicking their beaks. Starts at

London Bridge between *09.00 & 09.30*. Phone 071-236 1863 for details.
BR/Tube: London Bridge

AUGUST

Notting Hill Carnival
Notting Hill W11
081-964 0544
This carnival, claiming to be Europe's largest outdoor festival, is held over the August Bank holiday weekend, each day from *noon* to *early evening*. It started initially as a celebration of West Indian culture with traditional steel bands. As the event expanded, more bands from many areas of the world began to take part and the streets now become packed with entertainers and colourful costumes. Sunday is carnival day for the children with their parade of costume bands. The main procession and adult bands are on Monday. There are also three special stages where top international groups appear throughout the day. Apart from all the lively music, there are over 150 stalls in the area selling a marvellous mixture of West Indian and African food as well as handicrafts, T-shirts, records and tapes.
Free
Tube: Notting Hill Gate, Ladbroke Grove

Autumn (September/October/November)

SEPTEMBER

National Fun Run
Hyde Park W2
081-940 5221 (recorded information)
This 2½ mile charity run takes place in either late September or early October. Hundreds of so-called 'fun runners' enter in age groups from 8 to 80. Although it is principally an event for individuals, there are placings for teams and families. For further details write to: PO Box 58, Richmond, Surrey TW9 1TX.
Charge
Tube: Knightsbridge, Hyde Park Corner, Lancaster Gate

OCTOBER

Annual Full Tidal Closure
Thames Barrier Visitors' Centre, Unity Way, Eastmoor Street, Woolwich SE18
081-854 1373
The annual closing of the Thames Barrier takes place for one day during October. The checks last about eight hours and during this time it's possible to see the barriers lifting out of the water. When there is no action, the exhibition at the Visitors Centre is well worth a browse. There are also monthly closures, though these

don't last as long. Contact the centre for the closure days as they vary from month to month.
Charge for Visitors Centre, free for watching barriers
Tube: New Cross, New Cross Gate   *BR:* Charlton

Punch & Judy Fellowship Festival
Covent Garden Piazza WC2
081-802 4656 (Professor Percy Press II)
Punch & Judy was first introduced to Covent Garden in 1662 so it is an appropriate venue for this all-day festival. The Punch & Judy Fellowship consists of over 150 members and they stage a continuous show on the first Sunday in October from *10.30-17.30*.
Free
Tube: Covent Garden

NOVEMBER
Guy Fawkes Night Fireworks
Bonfires and firework displays are put on in several London parks. A huge bonfire is built on Primrose Hill where there are splendid views of the lights of London. A half hour display is also put on in Battersea Park at around *20.00*.
Free
Primrose Hill: *Tube:* Camden Town
Battersea Park: *Tube:* Sloane Square (then by bus 137)
               BR: Battersea Park

Lord Mayor's Show
City of London
071-606 3030
The Lord Mayor of London travelling in a state coach with around 140 floats processes from Guildhall through the City to arrive at the Law Courts in the Strand WC2 at around *11.50*. Then on to Mansion House, Walbrook EC4, the official residence of the Lord Mayor. This occasion is the biggest ceremonial event in the City.
Free
Tube: Bank

Remembrance Sunday
This service takes place each year on the second Sunday in November at *11.00* at the Cenotaph in Whitehall SW1. Begun after the First World War, the servicemen lost in the two World Wars are remembered with a salute of guns. Poppies are also sold in the street to raise money for ex-servicemen. For further information contact 071-930 4466.

Winter (December/January/February)

DECEMBER
Carol Singing
Trafalgar Square WC2. From the second week of December there

are carols recorded on tape in the Square from early evening. Join in the singing or just listen!
Free
Tube/BR: Charing Cross

Christmas Lights
The Christmas lights in Regent Street and Oxford Street are ceremoniously turned on by a celebrity guest at the beginning of December.
Free
Tube: Piccadilly Circus, Oxford Circus

New Year's Eve
Trafalgar Square WC2.
Traditional revelry to bring in the New Year takes place in Trafalgar Square with the singing of *Auld Land Syne* by massed crowds and dancing around the fountains.
Free
Tube: Charing Cross

JANUARY

Chinese New Year Festival
Chinatown, Gerrard St W1
071-437 5256 (Chinatown Chinese Association)
In the heart of the West End is Chinatown, the setting for the Chinese New Year celebrations. It's a noisy, colourful affair with papier mâché dragons weaving amongst the crowds, food and craft stalls, and many gorgeous costumes to see.
Free
Tube: Leicester Square

Lord Mayor of Westminster's New Year's Day Parade
081-992 9600
Follow the bands to Hyde Park for a lively afternoon's entertainment. Since its first performance in 1986, this is one of the largest parades in Europe with some 5000 performers. There is everything from marching bands and cheer leaders to colourful floats and veteran vehicles. Starts at *12.30* in Piccadilly W1.
Free
Tube: Green Park, Piccadilly Circus

WATERWAYS

Canals

London's canals are easily overlooked, but these miles of waterways with their towpaths running alongside provide many opportunities for outdoor activities.

The Grand Union, Regent's and Hertford Union canals sweep through London in a wide arc, linking up with the River Thames to the south and the River Lee to the east. Two hundred years ago, the canal network proved essential to the rapid development of the port of London. The first canal was opened in 1793. It ran from Brentford Locks, on the Thames, to Uxbridge. Another arm of the Grand Union from Southall to Paddington was opened in 1801, and the Regent's Canal, connecting Paddington Basin to the Thames at Limehouse was completed in 1820. Initially the canals were a commercial success carrying coal, timber, corn, hay and even chocolate, but the advent of the railways meant strong competition and trade fell away. In recent years the canals have undergone a major revival. Towpaths have been renewed and there are many access points along the way, often near bus stops or tube stations. More seating, extra picnic places and boat club facilities have all been created.

Apart from being a good place to walk, there are a number of regular boat trips on the canals and mooring points for those with their own boats. Swimming is prohibited. Some cycling is allowed but a licence is required and fishing is restricted to permit holders. For more details, leaflets and information sheets on London's canals contact: Waterways Manager, British Waterways, London's Waterways, Delamere Terrace, Little Venice, London W2 6ND. 071-482 0523.

In this section, you'll find details of canal conservation work, walks and cruises. For details of boat and canoe clubs, look in the appropriate watersport sections.

Canal campaigns

Inland Waterways Association
114 Regent's Park Road NW1
071-586 2510/2556
The Inland Waterways Association (IWA) was formed over 40 years ago when many of Britain's canals and waterways were

either abandoned or derelict and in danger of disappearing for ever. The IWA campaigns to improve and expand the existing waterway network, and organises events along canals throughout the country. The Waterway Recovery Group, also based at the Regent's Park Road office, is the national co-ordinating body for voluntary labour on the inland waterways. Contact them if you are interested in canal conservation.

Guided walks along the canal

Inland Waterways Association
114 Regent's Park Road NW1
071-586 2510/2556
The Inland Waterways Association (IWA) leads two towpath walks on Regent's Canal. Both start in Camden. One goes up the canal to Little Venice and the other down towards the Islington Tunnel. The walks last about two hours. There is a charge which is used to help keep Britain's canals alive.
Where to go: Meet at Camden Town tube station.
Times: Between Feb & Nov first Sunday of every month at 14.30 and Tue at 18.30.
Charge

Ramblers' Association (London Area)
29 Redcliffe Close, Old Brompton Road SW5
The Ramblers, in association with British Waterways, organise a summer programme of walks along the canals. The rambles last about two hours and allow time for everyone to have a drink in the pub afterwards. In addition to the afternoon and evening strolls

there are some special all-day family events on a Sunday. No need to book. For details phone the British Waterways Canal Office: 071-482 0523 or contact the Ramblers' Association at the above address.
Where to go: Meeting places are at BR or tube stations.
Times: Mar-Sep 14.30 Sat, 18.45 Wed.
Free

Self-guided walks along the canal

A booklet and map available from the London Tourist Board (071-730 3488) shows some of the walks that are possible along London's canals. There are 54 miles of towpath with only a few short breaks at the Islington Tunnel, Maida Vale and Limehouse Cut. Route finding is not difficult. One of the most popular sections is the 2½ mile stretch from Camden Town to Little Venice. The section from Camden to the Thames is also very interesting, or you can venture further west from Little Venice through attractive parts such as Horsenden Hill and Osterley Park.

Canal trips

These trips are not strictly speaking 'outdoor London' as passengers on the narrowboats travel under cover, but it is a relaxing way to experience the waterways. The section between Little Venice and Camden is most popular with tourists. Those living in London may like to go further afield; for example to the Colne Valley.

Colne Valley Passengerboat Services
Denham Marina, 100 Acres, Sandersons Road, Uxbridge, Middlesex (0895) 812130
Operating on the Grand Union Canal between Brentford and Rickmansworth, at the foot of the Chilterns, these cruises go through the lovely Colne Valley Country Park. Along the way are many historical canal features including the deepest lock on the Grand Union. Phone for details of special all-day trips, jazz cruises and private charters.
Where to go: Start from the Swan & Bottle, Oxford Road, Uxbridge.
Times: Easter-end Sep 14.45 Sun & Wed.
Charge
Tube: Uxbridge

The Floating Boater
1 Bishop's Bridge Road W2
071-724 8740
Phone for details of the charter trips organised by this firm on *Lapwing*, one of Britain's oldest traditional narrowboats, and *The Prince Regent*. The cruises go along Regent's Park to Camden Lock and the four locks beyond to Battlebridge Basin.

Where to go: Start from North Wharf Road W2.
Times: phone for details as times vary.
Charge
BR/Tube: Paddington

Jason's Trip
Little Venice W9
071-286 3428
Jason, once a hard-working narrowboat, now runs from Little Venice through Regent's Park as far as Camden Lock. There is a chance to get off there and explore the open-air craft shops and flea market which is open Saturday & Sunday. The trip lasts 1½ hours.
Where to go: The mooring is opposite 60 Blomfield Road W9.
Times: Apr-Oct 10.30, 12.30 & 14.30 Mon-Sun.
Charge
Tube: Warwick Avenue

Jenny Wren Cruises
250 Camden High Street NW1
071-485 4433/6210
The *Jenny Wren*, a traditionally-designed and decorated narrow-boat, cruises along the Regent's Canal from Camden Town to Little Venice. The journey lasts about 1½ hours. Mystery tours go to unusual parts of the canal with stops for refreshments at canalside pubs. There are occasional dock trips down to the Thames at Limehouse. Luxury evening cruises are available on *My Fair Lady* when a three-course meal is served.
Where to go: Cruises leave from Garden Jetty, 250 Camden High Street NW1.
Times: Mar-Oct 11.30 (except Sat), 14.00 & 15.30 Mon-Sun.
Charge
Tube: Camden Town

Regent's Canal Waterbus
London Waterbus Company
Little Venice, Blomfield Road, Maida Vale W9 &
Camden Lock, Commercial Place, off Chalk Farm Road NW1
071-482 2550
This company runs trips along Regent's Canal westwards to Little Venice through Regent's Park, with a chance to stop at London Zoo. The route east goes to King's Cross, Islington and Bow. There are also occasional trips up the River Lea.
Where to go: Little Venice - mooring on Warwick Crescent W9.
                Camden Lock - mooring on Camden Lock Pier NW1.
Times: Both trips *Mar 31-Sep 30 departures hourly 10.00-17.00 Mon-Sun.*
Charge
Tube: Warwick Avenue for Little Venice trip
Tube: Camden Town for Camden Lock trip

River transport

Riverbus
The Chambers, Chelsea Harbour, Lots Road SW10
071-376 3676
These smart, modern launches tour the river at a surprisingly fast pace. Comfortable, spacious interiors make it a very pleasant way to travel. A good way to get to London Bridge City from upriver. The route goes from Chelsea Harbour to Greenwich Pier, stopping at Charing Cross, Festival Pier, Swan Lane Pier, London Bridge Pier, West India Pier and Greenland Pier.
Departures are *every 20 minutes between 07.00-10.00 & 16.00-19.00 Mon-Fri, every 30 minutes between 10.00-16.00 & 19.00-20.00 Mon-Fri and every 30 minutes from 10.00-18.00 Sat & Sun.*

River trips

There are river trips from up and down stream with occasional commentaries on the outward trip. These have a certain magic whether to old favourites such as Greenwich or Kew or the latest in modern technology – The Thames Barrier. Services are plentiful in the summer and restricted in the winter. The river breezes can get quite cold so wrap up well if you want to spend time on deck.
For recorded information on river trips phone 071-730 4812 or contact the Pier direct:

Charing Cross Pier
Victoria Embankment WC2
071-839 3572
To Greenwich and the Tower of London.
Charge
Tube: Embankment

Tower Pier
Tower Hill, London EC3
071-488 0344
To Westminster and Greenwich.
Charge
Tube: Tower Hill

Westminster Pier
Victoria Embankment SW1
Downstream to Greenwich (071-930 4097) and Tower Piers (071-930 9033). Upstream to Hampton Court, Kew, Putney and Richmond (071-930 2062/4721).
Charge
Tube: Westminster

The Thames Barrier

Thames Barrier Visitors Centre
Unity Way, Woolwich SE18
081-854 1373
The world's largest movable flood barrier spanning over 500 yards across the Thames. There are 10 separate steel gates and distinctive piers which house the hydraulic machinery. The best time to go is during its monthly raising. Phone the centre for dates and times. At the centre is an exhibition with working models of the barrier and an audiovisual presentation of London's history. Nearby is a picnic area so you can make the most of a day trip.
Open: 10.30-17.00 Mon-Fri, 10.30-17.30 Sat & Sun.
Tube: New Cross, New Cross Gate   *BR:* Charlton

Round-Barrier Boat Cruise
081-854 5555
Short cruises are run from Barrier Gardens Pier, lasting about half an hour with a full commentary on the Barrier and local geography. There are also longer cruises direct from Westminster Pier (1¼ hours), Tower Pier (1 hour) or Greenwich (½ hour). These stop at the Barrier so there's a chance to look round the exhibition.
Services run from *Easter-Oct (with limited winter service) Mon-Sun.*
From Barrier Gardens Pier: *every 30 minutes from 10.00-16.00.*
From Westminster Pier: *every 45 minutes from 10.00-15.15.*
From Tower Pier: *11.15, 13.30 & 15.30.*
From Greenwich: *every 1¼ hours from 11.15.*

SPORTS

THERE is a vast number of outdoor sporting activities in London, from athletics to windsurfing. Below are listed some useful general addresses:

London Playing Fields Society
Boston Manor Playing Fields, Boston Gardens, Brentford, Essex
081-560 3667
This body is responsible for administering the largest number of playing fields in the London area. If you are a club looking for a ground, they can probably help you out. If you are an individual wanting to see various sports in action, they can let you know what is going on at local pitches.

The main grounds are at Boston Manor (also the administrative offices), Fairlop, Barkingside and Prince George's, Merton. The flagship site consisting of a sports centre and 33 acres of pitches is the Douglas Eyre Sports Centre, Coppermill Lane, Walthamstow E17. 081-520 4918. This is also a centre of excellence and they aim to extend PE in the schools through to adult life as well as helping newcomers take up sports. Courses are held for those wanting to become coaches.

London Sports Club for the Blind
34 Lanacre Avenue, Graham Park Estate NW9
081-521 3359
The aim of the sports club is to facilitate the provision of sporting and recreational facilities for the blind and partially-sighted. These include making special arrangements in each sport such as providing sighted assistants to keep runners on the track in athletics, or a system of guiding strings in bowls to enable those who are visually handicapped to participate.

Metropolitan Sports & Social Club for the Visually Handicapped
29 Gilda Court, Watford Way NW7
(Secretary: Derek Mileman)
081-203 1286 (answerphone)
This club was founded in 1973 with the aim of providing better provision of sports and social facilities for the visually handicapped in the Greater London area. In its first year, the major activities were football, cricket, swimming and athletics. Since then the range has increased to include skating, skiing, fencing and

judo. The club can also provide information and contact points on a wide range of activities from archery to weight-training.

Outdoor Activities Initiative
72 St John Street EC1
071-490 4051
The Outdoor Activities Initiative (OAI) aims to increase participation by Londoners in outdoor activities. It provides a network linking the various agencies which provide outdoor facilities and expertise with the many different groups and individuals using the outdoors. They are pleased to help with individual activities. OAI also provide a free map showing outdoor activity venues.

Sports Council
16 Upper Woburn Place WC1
071-388 1277
The Sports Council was set up by Royal Charter in 1972 with four main aims. Firstly to encourage participation in sports, secondly to increase facilities for sport, thirdly to promote excellence in sport both in terms of performance and behaviour and finally to provide information for groups and individuals.

On the ball

I have heard it said that the British invent sports; when we begin to lose at existing ones we simply invent a new one. And a great proportion of them employ a ball! There is certainly now an enormous variety of ball sports to choose from, each offering something different in thrills, skills and tactics.

Baseball

There are now some 70 teams playing baseball in the London area. They play both in formal leagues and at informal meetings in places such as Hyde Park and Regent's Park.

Baseball is a nine-a-side game which has long been regarded as one of America's national games. It is similar in style to rounders, which many British will have played on summer afternoons. A game called Base Ball was played in both Britain and America in the 18th century, but the Americans take the credit for originating the modern game.

It is played on a field containing four bases known as a diamond. The object is to score runs by hitting the ball and getting round the bases before being put out. It is a game that demands some eye and hand co-ordination, especially for the batsmen, and good throwing techniques from the fieldsmen. The game is open to all ages and both sexes though it seems to attract more men than women. It is particularly known for encouraging a wide range of tactical plays.

How to start & where to learn
Baseball clubs welcome novices. There is usually a weekly training session lasting 1-2 hours where you can practise some of the necessary skills and learn the rules. It is best to go to several training sessions to see how you get on. The advantage of baseball is that you don't necessarily have to be an all-rounder and players are positioned on the field according to their strengths. To find out about your local team contact: Sarah Collins (Secretary), The British Baseball Federation, 193a Bellegrove Road, Welling, Kent DA16 3RA. 081-856 4429. Under 15s should contact Bob Locke, 107 Ware Road, Hoddesdon, Hertfordshire EN11 9AE. (0992) 442202. There are only a few junior teams, but some senior clubs may start junior teams if there is enough interest.

Where to play
Many of London's parks, especially Hyde Park and Regent's Park.

Softball

There are three types of softball - fast pitch, medium pitch and soft pitch, which is the most popular in London. Like baseball, softball is played on a diamond, and the skills needed are catching, throwing, batting and base running. Pitching (bowling) is different in that the ball is thrown under arm. The ball is larger than the one used in baseball and far from soft! The game was developed initially as an indoor version of baseball using a smaller pitch, but as it grew in popularity it moved outside. Mixed teams are a feature of the sport.

There is a Greater London mixed league as well as men's and women's and business leagues. Matches are played on summer weekday evenings as well as weekends.

How to start & where to learn
The best way to start is to turn up at Regent's Park on a Sunday afternoon where there are numerous games in progress. Some are league matches but many of the games are casual and the players very friendly. Ask to have a go and you'll probably be lent a bat and given a basic idea of the rules. After a few sessions, you can find a team that suits you. Some train seriously, others remain informal.

Where to play
London's parks, especially Regent's Park.

Bowls

Bowling is a sport which is getting younger. Once the province of the retired, there are now junior sections (under 25s) and the competitive senior classes are led by the under 60s. It is a sport, however, that can be enjoyed at any age as it doesn't have to be very physical. It helps to be supple to get a good flowing action and to be able to bend the knees. There are fixed stances for those with stiffer joints. Good hand to eye co-ordination is needed to judge the line and distance to the jack. The basic idea can be learnt quite quickly for those wanting to enjoy a casual game, but there are also subtleties which are learnt with experience. Interesting situations develop depending on the number of balls on the green. It is not always just a question of getting near the jack, in case another bowler knocks it out of the way. Good bowlers have to be able to foresee several moves ahead.

How to start & where to learn

The English Bowling Association publishes a small booklet with general guidelines for new bowlers (small charge). Write to the English Bowling Association, Lyndhurst Road, Worthing, West Sussex BN11 2AZ. (0903) 820222. They also run a coaching scheme covering the various disciplines such as indoor and outdoor bowling and variations using a crown green.

Joining a club is another good way to begin. Contact the English Bowling Association or one of the following secretaries to find out what is available locally. They should also be able to give advice on coaching schemes.

Essex:
E.G.Redgwell, 52 Winchester Avenue, Cranham, Upminster, Essex RM14 3LR. (04022) 27358.

Kent:
M.G.Bannister, 153 Colyer Road, Northfleet, Kent DA11 8AZ. (0474) 356811.

Middlesex
D.H.Dorling, 6 Ellington Court, High Street, Southgate N14. 081-886 6384.

Surrey
A.S.Ballantyne, 150 Meadow Walk, Ewell Court, Ewell, Surrey KT19 0BA. 081-393 3938.

Where to play

Apart from privately owned bowling greens, there are several public greens in London's parks.
Battersea Park SW11. 081-871 7530.
Brockwell Park SE24. 081-674 6141.
Clissold Park N16. 071-254 9736.
Danson Park, Bexleyheath, Kent. 081-303 7777.
Dulwich Park SE21. 081-693 5737.

Petanque

Petanque is the proper name for the French game of boules. It has grown in popularity here in the last 20 years and especially since the staging of the world championship in 1979. It is easily learned and can be enjoyed by the whole family. Another attraction is the element of chance involved because of the uneven terrain on which it is played. This means a beginner can have a close game with a more experienced player.

Petanque is played with metal boules which weigh just over a pound each. In singles and doubles the players use three boules each, in triples, two boules. The first player throws the cochonnet (similar to a jack) between 6m and 10m away and then throws a boule as close to it as possible. The next player tries to throw his boule nearer the cochonnet or to knock away the leading boule. The boule nearest the cochonnet leads. The team which is not leading continues to throw either until they have a leading boule or until there are no boules left. The team which ends up with the most boules nearest the cochonnet wins. Count one point for each boule nearest the cochonnet. The winners are the first team to reach thirteen points.

How to start & where to learn
Once you have the equipment it is easy to play casually. There are a few registered clubs in London which play petanque, and more outside London. For more details contact: Garth Freeman, National Administrator, British Petanque Association, PO Box 87, Leatherhead, Surrey KT22 8LA. (0372) 386860.

Where to play
There are no special terrains as such. Any gravelled surface is suitable.

Croquet

The myth that croquet is more of a genteel diversion than a sport still persists. It is in fact a skilful tactical game with the best players able to think seven or eight moves ahead.

Croquet is played by two or four players with four different coloured balls; blue, black, red and yellow. The aim is to be the first to get through the six hoops on the lawn in one direction, to return, and then to finish by hitting the central peg. The rules of the game allow you to hit the balls of the opponent, not just to bash them out of the way, but to position them to your advantage. A roquet shot is where the striker's ball hits one of the other players' balls. The striker is then allowed two more shots. In the first, the croquet stroke, the striker places his ball against the roqueted ball and sends it to a position that will be useful to him further on (whether or not it is 'useful' to his victim!). Then he is allowed a shot with his own ball. In this shot he may be able to roquet another ball, or make a hoop. Either means he can continue as striker. It may sound simple but the strategy can be quite complicated and fascinating. Croquet is a game suitable for a wide age range where players can compete on more or less equal terms.

How to start & where to learn
Whilst it may seem easy to hit the ball round the lawn, it is worth understanding the complexities of the sport to get the most out of this game. It is best to get advice from an experienced player or attend one of the Croquet Association's courses, though these are not necessarily in London.

There are a number of clubs in the London area, most of which welcome beginners and many have coaches. For a complete list of local clubs contact Brian MacMillan at the Croquet Association, The Hurlingham Club, Ranelagh Gardens, London SW6 3PR. 071-736 3148. He will also send free literature about the game.

Where to play
There are no public croquet grounds in or out of London. You must join a club to gain access to a ground.

Golf

Golf is a game enjoyed by millions of people throughout the world. Television coverage of major tournaments has increased its popularity, and its appeal to a younger age group. It doesn't require great athletic ability. The challenge lies in controlling the ball over long and short distances and specially-designed terrains.

Clothing & equipment
Fourteen is the maximum number of clubs that can be carried round a course. A basic set of five clubs can be enough for a beginner. You will also need a bag to carry the clubs, plus golf balls, tee pegs and waterproof clothing. A pair of golf shoes which give a good grip on the ground is essential. As a course is often over 5 miles, get a pair that fit well. Special shoes are not necessary on a driving range.

How to start & where to learn
If you have never played golf before, get tuition from a qualified professional teacher. These teachers are members of the Professional Golfers Association (PGA). All courses and clubs have a resident professional attached who can give advice and lessons.

Alternatively, another way to learn is to contact your local borough. Many of these run winter classes (often inside) where you can learn some basic skills. There are also driving ranges around London, which are good places to practise.

The Golf Foundation
57 London Road, Enfield, Middlesex EN2 6DU
081-367 4404
This is the national body responsible for the promotion and development of junior golf. The Foundation can help with tuition fees and awards vouchers to promising youngsters. They also publish a

small booklet *Taking up Golf* with guidelines on how to start, rules, equipment and so on.

Regent's Park Golf & Tennis School
Outer Circle, Regent's Park, London NW1 4RL
071-724 0643
Has facilities for tuition for absolute beginners through to advanced players on putting greens and bunkers. They can also give you information on where to play. There is also a 'made to measure' club service.
Open: 08.00-21.00 Mon-Sun.

Where to play
Incredible though it may seem, one of the hardest things about golf is getting to play on a course in the first place. On some busy public golf courses, it is a case of booking a round at *03.00* or *04.00* during the summer. Clubs usually have less busy courses, and although there are often steep fees for joining, it can be good value if you play frequently. Bear in mind that there are long waiting lists at most clubs, but occasionally new developments advertise for members in golfing magazines.

Public Courses
Essex:
Clayhill Lane, Sparrow's Hearn, Kingswood, Basildon.
(0268) 533297.
Belhus Park Municipal, Belhus Park, South Ockenden.
(0708) 854260.
158 Station Road, Chingford E4. 081-529 2107.
Fairlop Waters, Forest Road, Barkingside, Ilford. 081-500 9911.
Chigwell Row, Hainault Forest. 081-500 2097.
Risebridge Chase, Lower Bedfords Road, Romford. (0708) 41429.
Royal Epping Forest, Forest Approach, Station Road, Chingford E4.
081-529 6407. (Red coats or trousers compulsory).
Kent:
Braeside, The Mansion, Beckenham Palace Park, Beckenham.
081-650 2292.
Magpie Hall Lane, Bromley. 081-462 7014.
Middlesex:
Church Road, Hanwell W7. 081-567 1287.
The Drive, Harefield Place, Uxbridge. (0895) 31169.
Horsenden Hill, Woodland Rise, Greenford. 081-902 4555.
Staines Road, Hounslow Heath. 081-570 5271.
Lime Trees Park, Ruislip Road, Northolt. 081-845 3180.
Perivale Park, Ruislip Road, Greenford. 081-575 8655.
Picketts Lock, Picketts Lock Lane, Edmonton N9. 081-803 3611.
Ickenham Road, Ruislip. (0895) 632004/638081.
Trent Park, Bramley Road, Southgate N14. 081-366 7432.
Staines Road, Twickenham. 081-979 6946.
Whitewebbs, Beggars Hollow, Clay Hill, Enfield. 081-363 2951.
Surrey:
Addington Court, Featherbed Lane, Addington, Croydon.
081-657 0281/2/3.
Chessington Golf Centre, Garrison Lane, Chessington.
081-391 0948.
Coulsdon Court, Coulsdon Road, Coulsdon, Croydon.
081-660 0468.
Richmond Park (Roehampton Gate) SW15. 081-876 3205.

Tennis

Wimbledon fortnight is one of the great spectator events of the year. Despite its popularity, the myth still remains that tennis is a rather elitist sport played in expensive clubs. This is far from true. The best known clubs such as Queen's and Hurlingham do have long waiting lists, but there are 325 other tennis clubs to choose from in the London area as well as over 2000 public tennis courts. There is ample opportunity for anyone to take up this sport.

How to start & where to learn

To get involved in tennis, several choices are available. First you can simply join a club. The advantage of this is that clubs have good quality courts and you will soon meet others who are interested in the game. There are usually social and clubhouse facilities on offer. There may, however, be waiting lists and some clubs may require a playing test before membership is agreed. Check out a club by visiting it first. Ask about membership fees as these vary considerably.

A less well-known way to get involved is to contact your local borough. There is an outstanding centre at Bishops Park SW6 (071-736 1354) and a junior centre in Rosehill Park, Rosehill Road, Sutton, Surrey (081-641 6611). Most boroughs have a coach and offer a range of coaching activities using local courts, including courses for beginners, juniors, seniors, over 50s, women only and short tennis. Several boroughs run Ratings Tournaments - a new concept where players are given a category according to their standard of play and only players with similar ratings play each other.

A third option is to join the Lawn Tennis Association (LTA). Membership is open to everyone from armchair enthusiasts to aspiring professionals. It gives you automatic entry to the Wimbledon Ticket Ballot as well as a national rating and eligibility to play in the singles at LTA Official Tournaments.

Where to play

There are over 2000 public courts in the London area and all London boroughs have a reasonable number of courts, some more than 100. If popular places are booked up there is usually an alternative venue. Charges for hiring courts can be cheap though it varies from borough to borough. For a complete list of clubs and public courts contact Danielle Lewis, London Development Officer, Lawn Tennis Association Trust, Queen's Club, Palliser Road W14. 071-385 4233.

Perfect pitch

Games such as cricket, football, rugby and to a lesser extent hockey are all well known. Common to all these games is the fact that they are seldom taken up by adults but tend to be played by anyone who has played at school. Novices and beginners are welcomed, juniors perhaps more so than the geriatric over thirties! There are plenty of opportunities to get involved in these sports wherever you live in London and whether you are male or female.

Cricket

Cricket as a game has evolved over centuries. It began on village greens, particularly in the agricultural south during the 17th century, and then spread throughout England. However, the hub of the game still remained in the south with the establishment of the MCC (Marylebone Cricket Club) in the 1790s. Although at times slow moving, its complexities can make it hard to follow. In its simplest form it is a game played by two teams of eleven. One side bats, scoring runs, while the other team fields and tries to get the batsmen out.

How to start & where to learn

If you have a yearning to have a go at cricket (male or female) but have always felt it only really belongs in the realms of the ex-public school brigade, all neatly turned out in white, then you could get involved in one of the many schemes set up by the London Community Cricket Association (LCCA), 160 Wyndham Road, London SE5 0UB. 071-708 1686. This body was founded in 1984 with the aim of making cricket accessible to a wide range of people by introducing them to informal games, and by organising coaching courses and coached games. The LCCA have started a number of leagues who play fairly informal games on mid-week evenings. These are either 7- or 8- aside teams.

The LCCA also try to encourage youngsters by making contacts and finding qualified coaches in a number of boroughs where there are facilities as well as organising matches. Many of these sessions are free, and you don't need equipment as everything is provided.

Where to play

London may not have many village greens, but there are many local clubs who play in county leagues. These clubs are principally for those who have already wielded a bat or thrown a ball. Some clubs do offer coaching for beginners. To get in touch with a local club, contact Club Cricket Conference, 353 West Barnes Lane, New Malden, Surrey. 081-949 4001. If you are already in a team and short of fixtures, Club Cricket Conference can fix up matches. (There is a small affiliation charge). They have some 1500 members in the London area and also produce a handbook listing clubs.

Alternatively, contact the National Cricket Association (NCA), Lord's Cricket Ground, St John's Wood Road NW8. 071-286 4766. They can help individuals find a local club and will also give advice to beginners on where they can get coaching.

Women's cricket

There are a dozen or so women's teams who play at grounds spread around London. It is best to join these teams if you already play. For details contact the LCCA.

There are also opportunities to go on winter courses (held indoors) and then play outside in June and July with the benefit of specially-coached games. For details contact the LCCA.

For general information on the organisation and structure of women's cricket contact: The Administration Officer, The Women's Cricket Association, The Yorkshire Cricket School, 41 St Michael's Lane, Headingley, Leeds LS6 3BR. (0532) 742398.

Cricket for the Blind

This is played with a larger ball, filled with ball bearings so it can be heard as it travels through the air. There are some variations on the rules. For example the definition of a catch is altered so that the ball may bounce once or twice before being caught. I'm told that the blind teams often win against a sighted opposition. For information on these games contact the Metropolitan Sports and Social Club for the Visually Handicapped: 081-203 1286 or Roger Clifton at the London Sports Club for the Blind: 081-521 3359.

Football

Football at a professional level may have had its ups and downs but at local level it is alive and kicking. There are hundreds of clubs around London. Games are played in many of the parks on Saturdays, Sundays and mid-week.

How to start & where to learn

If you can kick a ball you can play. Simply trot down to your local park and see if there is a match on - much of it gets started by word of mouth. Usually there are officials on the touch line who will tell you about the clubs playing, training sessions and so on. If you are in a club and looking for matches, contact the London Football Association, Aldworth Grove, London SE13 6HY. 081-690 9626. They also organise leagues and competitions in London.

There are over 60 clubs for women in the Greater London area from the Hampstead Heathens to the Vicarage Wanderers. For a list of clubs and details of national fixtures for several months ahead, write to the Women's Football Association, 450 Hanging Ditch, Corn Exchange, Manchester M4 3ES. 061-832 5911.

Where to play

There are many football pitches in the London area both in the parks as well as at purpose-built recreation grounds. It is also worth contacting the London Playing Fields Society (see page 76).

Hockey

Schoolgirl memories of muddy pitches or what seemed like hours shivering on the right wing may still be vivid, but they don't prevent a large section of the population continuing with this sport into adult life. Hockey is also no longer such a predominantly female sport. The number of male clubs through the country almost equals the women's ones.

How to start & where to learn
Many will have played at school and so few people take up this sport from scratch in adult life, except in the case of men who may have been invalided out of rugby! There is limited help for absolute beginners, so it is best to go along and watch a couple of matches to see if you'll enjoy playing. The best way to start is to join a club - some may have coaching and will probably run training sessions to help with general skills, rules and fitness. Junior novices are welcomed. Clubs do not expect to provide equipment and sticks, although beginners may be lent a stick for the first few sessions.
Men should contact: The Hockey Association, 18 Northdown Street N1. 071-837 8878.
Women should contact: The All England Women's Hockey Association, 51 High Street, Shrewsbury, Shropshire SY1 1ST. (0743) 233572.
Although based outside London, the association will give a list of London clubs, plus the name of a territorial or regional secretary who can tell you more about local teams.

Where to play
Matches are played at weekends in many parts of London in the parks and recreation grounds. It is also worth contacting the London Playing Fields Society (see page 76).

Rugby League

The first game of Rugby League was recorded in 1895, when exasperated northerners made a break from Rugby Union and founded the Northern Union. The name was changed in 1922 to Rugby Football League but the game has always had a strong northern bias. Fans claim that it is a better game than Rugby Union, demanding more strength and speed and offering more to the players. Progress is generally made by running with the ball rather than by kicking. The ball can stay in play for three quarters of the game meaning players are constantly on the go. It is a demanding, physical sport for which you need to be robust and fit.

How to start & where to learn

Rugby League clubs welcome any new members whether they be northern exiles who have played the game at school or deserters from Rugby Union! The season runs from September to May. Players are not allowed to change clubs mid season nor join a club after January 31st. Most clubs train at least once a week.

For details of the London clubs and the Amateur Rugby League contact Paul Spencer-Thompson (secretary), London Amateur Rugby League, 24 Clanricarde Gardens W2. 071-792 0469.

Where to play

Bexleyheath RC: Hall Place, Bourne Road, Bexleyheath, Kent. *Kick Off: 11.00*

Ealing RC: Northwick Park, Wembley, Middlesex. *Kick Off: 11.00*

Fulham Travellers, Merton RUFC, Morden Recreation Ground, Middleton Road, St Helier, Surrey. *Kick Off: 11.00*

London Colonials, Hurlingham Park Stadium, Hurlingham Road, Fulham SW6. *Kick Off: 13.00*

Peckham RC: Orchard School Playing Fields, William Booth Road, Annerley SE19. *Kick Off: 11.00*

South London Wanderers: London New Zealand RUFC, Jersey Road, Osterley, Middlesex. *Kick Off: 14.30*

St Mary's RC: St Mary's College, Waldegrave Road, Strawberry Hill, Twickenham, Middlesex. *Kick Off: 14.00*

Rugby Union

Rugby was first played at the eponymous public school. From there it was carried to the Universities and later to the clubs in Richmond and Blackheath who were responsible for organising it into the game that is known today. It is a 15 a-side game played with an oval ball. Rugby is usually played on a soft grass pitch which can quickly turn to mud after rain. It can be hard to tell the players from the pitch! The aim in rugby is to score tries (where the ball is carried over the defending team's goal line) and goals. The ball can be kicked in any direction, but it can only be passed backwards. Rugby is a hard physical game where possession of the ball is gained through tackling individuals or by a struggle between the forwards during a line out or a scrum. There is also opportunity to use a variety of tactics with dodging and dummy throws. There can be an exhilarating fluidity (both for spectators and players) when the ball is passed between the forwards and great excitement when one individual manages to outrun and pass the defence and hurl himself over the line to score a try.

The season runs from 1st September to mid-May but most clubs hold pre-season training and trials in August. Matches are usually played on Saturday afternoons. *Kick off is at 15.00.*

How to start & where to learn
Most adults who play Rugby Union have already had some experience of the game, usually at school. If you are coming back to the sport after a break, phone the Rugby Football Union (RFU), Whitton Road, Twickenham, Middlesex. 081-892 8161. They can can put you in touch with London's Divisional Technical Administrator who will then advise you on a club suited to your abilities. If you are a junior, the RFU have details of clubs with junior sections. There is also a Youth Development Officer who can be contacted at the RFU.

Where to play
There are a number of amateur teams based in the London area. Contact the London Rugby Football Exchange, 353 West Barnes Lane, New Malden, Surrey. 081-949 1881/2848, who have details of over 350. They will also help direct individuals to a local club as well as organise matches for affiliated teams.

In the air

Rise up in the world with the sports of ballooning, climbing and parascending! It is possible to get experience of all three of these activities within London, though the best venues are further afield. Although quite different in nature, all three are club-based. Joining a club is a good way to make contact with others who are interested, and to get tips from experts.

Ballooning

Imagine floating in an open wicker basket just six inches over a cornfield or 3000 feet up in the air. No wonder ballooning has

been described as the ultimate aerial experience. Ballooning is a relatively expensive sport, but by joining a balloon club it can be made considerably cheaper. Being a passenger is the easy bit. The only thing that might concern the pilot is your weight! If you want to become a balloon pilot, getting a licence is compulsory, and involves putting in a certain number of hours per year. Apart from learning how to handle the balloon; navigation, knowledge of the weather and ground crewing are all part of the training.

Clothing & equipment
Wear comfortable, casual clothes, a pair of strong gloves and flat shoes. Wellington boots are best in wet weather. It is useful to have extra layers to put on (or strip off). Surprisingly it may be warmer in the balloon than on the ground!

How to start & where to learn
There is a London-based club for enthusiasts and novices alike. For more details contact the London Region of the British Balloon & Airship Club (LRBBAC) and the Capital Balloon Club (CBC), 18-19 Linhope Street NW1. 071-706 1021. They hold regular meetings on the last Wednesday of each month, with a guest speaker. Balloon meets are organised at these meetings. The CBC aims to promote excellence in the sport and encourage newcomers to fly. They offer introductory flights, training for a balloon licence, and hiring of balloons.

Where to go
Ballooning over London itself is severely restricted as balloons have to adhere to the rules in controlled air-space. Ballooning locations nearest to London are Havering and Brentwood in Essex and Potters Bar and Ware in Hertfordshire.

Mountaineering & climbing

Whilst there's no mountaineering as such in London, there are training facilities, climbing walls and clubs to help you get to grips with this activity. One advantage of this sport is that climbs come in a huge variety of standards from very simple and short to technically hard. There is probably something to suit everyone. The somewhat static nature of climbing means that unfit beginners can manage a short stretch, though to progress, strength, agility and overall fitness are increasingly important. It's thought by most people that a good sense of balance and no fear of heights are also essential, but apparently there are a number of good climbers who have neither of these attributes. Enthusiasts would encourage virtually anyone to have a go.

How to start & where to learn

The best way to learn is to join a club or go along to one of London's climbing walls. The clubs are not restricted to local activities, many have access to huts in climbing districts such as Snowdonia. For a list of clubs contact the British Mountaineering Council, Crawford House, Precinct Centre, Booth Street East, Manchester M13 9RZ. 061-273 5835.

Where to go

Although this is an outdoor sport, paradoxically the indoor climbing walls in London often provide more extensive and challenging facilities, after which you can progress to the great outdoors.

Brunel University Sports Centre

Kingston Lane, Uxbridge, Middlesex
(0895) 52361
This was the original indoor London climbing wall and still rates as one of the best in the country.
Open: 09.30-22.30 Mon-Fri (closed 17.00-19.00 Tue), 09.30-17.30 Sat & Sun.
Charge
BR/Tube: Uxbridge

North London Rescue Commando (NLRC)

Cordova Road E3
081-980 0289
Offering some of the most extensive indoor facilities in London, the inside of this huge old warehouse is given over exclusively to climbing walls. It is also a good place to see other climbers in action and pick up tips and advice on technique and equipment.
Open: 14.00-21.00 Tue, Wed, Thur & Fri, 10.00-17.00 Sat & Sun.
Charge
Tube: Mile End

Saddler's Sports Centre

Goswell Road EC1
071-253 9285
Outdoor wall. Affiliated to City University, so opening times may vary during the holidays. Phone to check.
Open: 09.30-21.30 Mon-Fri; Oct-Mar only 09.30-17.30 Sat, 11.00-17.00 Sun.
Charge
Tube: Angel, Farringdon

Sobell Sports Centre

Hornsey Road, Islington N7
071-609 2166 ·
Rated in the early eighties as the best indoor London climbing wall and still popular with many climbers. Check on opening times as they are liable to vary.
Open: 09.30-22.30 Mon-Fri, 09.30-21.00 Sat & Sun.
Charge
Tube: Holloway Road

Parascending

Parascending is one of the fastest growing air sports. Enthusiasts say it's one of the most exciting, and it has the advantage of being probably the least expensive in terms of equipment and getting airborne.

Parascenders are tow-launched into the air over land or water or foot-launched from a hillside. They can then soar like gliders in free flight. Once basic manoevres are mastered to give control over the flight, there are a whole range of advanced techniques to perfect. The parascender can attempt acrobatics such as spins and stalls, learn to land on a target the size of a 10p piece, or use the air flows to make a flight last literally for hours.

Clothing & equipment
All you need is a pair of ankle-supporting boots and over-clothes. Initially the rest of the gear - canopies, harness and helmet - can be borrowed.

How to start & where to learn
Clubs offer introductory courses in both flying and thorough ground training. These courses tend to last one day. After basic training, expert instructors can help with the more advanced aspects of flying. Check that the club you go to is a member of the British Association of Parascending Clubs. They provide licensed instructors who operate to strict safety guidelines. Insurance is part of the BAPC's membership which is essential in this risk sport. For further details contact the British Association of Paragliding Clubs, 18 Talbot Lane, Leicester LE1 4LR. (0533) 530318 (24hr answering service). They will provide a full information pack, directory of clubs, membership application form and copy of *Skywalker*, the parascending magazine.

Where to go
Brief details are listed below of clubs which operate near London. Please send an sae if you need more information on the types of courses run and costs.

The Brigade Parascending Club
Contact: Patrick Sugrue, Corran, Stees Way, Loughton, Essex. Tow-launching facilities at North Weald, Epping, as well as foot-launching on various hill sites. This club functions mainly at weekends. Introductory courses available on application.

Green Dragons Parascending Club
Contact: Andy Shaw, 9 Ballards Close, Dagenham, Essex RM10 9AP. This club operates at Wanstead Flats, near Ilford, Essex. There are flights all week. Introductory day courses offered as well as more advanced flying.

North Weald Parascending Club
Contact: Jim Grice, 32 Minton Heights, Rochford, Essex WS4 3EQ. Flying from North Weald, Epping on weekends and Bank holidays. Introductory courses on offer as well as 2-man dual training flights.

Sportlite Display Team
Contact: Brian Tripp, 181 Crystal Palace Road, East Dulwich SE22. Flights around South London and Brands Hatch, Kent. Individual training supplied on request.

One in front of the other

After the running boom in the eighties, it is not uncommon to see runners of all shapes, sizes and ages circling the parks and pounding the streets. Running and walking are good forms of exercise. Both tone the whole body. Running and walking raise the heartbeat, developing the heart muscle and improving levels of oxygen to the blood. Both sports are convenient and cheap. You can start from the minute you open your front door. Very little equipment is needed apart from investing in a good pair of shoes. Whilst running can be a solitary or individual activity, it also works well as a group sport. There are many running clubs throughout London where runners of all levels can meet and help each other train. There are also running-related sports such as Hash House Running and Orienteering which are fun to try. If you're keen on a slower pace, there are plenty of healthy rambles throughout the capital. See Parks on page 30 and Walks on page 40.

Athletics

Track and field events, known collectively as athletics, include a multitude of different activities all concerned with running, jumping or throwing. It is one of the oldest sports which started with the Olympic Games held in Ancient Greece. The first athletics contests in England were held in the 12th century.

Today, both television coverage, and medals won by British competitors at major events, have added a touch of glamour. British athletes excel at the track events but Fatima Whitbread, Tessa Sanderson, and Daley Thompson have all brought field events to the public's attention.

There are plenty of opportunities to take part in athletics. Over 650 clubs are listed in the southern counties of Essex, Kent, Middlesex and Surrey. Clubs that are known as Harriers tend to concentrate on running and road running (though there are exceptions to this rule) and athletics clubs train in both track and field events. Most clubs are for both men and women. If your children are keen to have a go, note that most clubs do not offer training to the under 11s as AAA rules forbid competition below that age.

Clothing & equipment

It is not necessary to have expensive equipment, not even spikes to start with, but you should wear proper training shoes.

How to start & where to learn

Beginners are welcomed into the sport. The best way to start is to turn up to club training for several sessions (there's often no obligation to join) and see how you get on. Athletics is a demanding discipline requiring suppleness, strength and stamina. These will only develop with training. Don't expect to break any records straight away, but there's still fun to be had having a go. To find out about a local club contact the Southern Counties Amateur Athletics Association, Suite 36, City of London Fruit Exchange, Brushfield Street E1. 071-247 2963.

If you want to take up a specific discipline such as launching yourself into space with a pole vault or swirling round with a shot putt, the Southern Counties AA will try to guide you to a club that has the necessary equipment and coaching facilities.

Where to go

There are a good number of all-weather tracks throughout London. These are often the meeting place for a local club. Facilities such as showers and changing rooms, weights room and indoor training areas vary. Floodlighting is often available for evening and winter training sessions. Below is a selection in the London area:

Bannister Stadium, Uxbridge Road, Harrow Weald, Middlesex. 081-428 7931.

Battersea Park, Albert Bridge Road SW11. 081-871 7537.

Copthall Stadium, Great North Way, Barnet NW4. 081-203 4211.

Croydon Sports Arena, Albert Road, South Norwood, Surrey. 081-654 3462.

Crystal Palace National Sports Centre, Ledrington Road SE19. 081-778 0131.

Erith Stadium, Avenue Road, Erith, Kent. 081-303 7777.

Hayes Stadium, Judge Heath Lane, Hayes, Middlesex. 081-573 0093.

Kingston Track, Kingston Road, Norbiton, Surrey. 081-547 2198.

New River Sports Centre, White Hart Lane, Wood Green N22. 081-881 2310.

Norman Park, Hayes Lane, Bromley, Kent. 081-462 5134.

Parliament Hill Fields, Highgate Road, Camden NW5. 071-435 8998.

Queen Elizabeth Stadium, Donkey Lane, Enfield, Middlesex. 081-363 7398.

Southwark Park, Jamaica Road SE16. 071-231 9442.

Terrence Macmillan Stadium, Maybury Road, Newham E13. 071-511 4477.

Tooting Track, Dr Johnson Avenue, Tooting Bec SW17. 081-871 7171.

West London Stadium, Du Cane Road, Hammersmith W12. 081-749 5505.

Wimbledon Park, Wimbledon Park Road, Merton SW18. 081-543 2222.

Running

Now the London Marathon is firmly established in the capital's calendar, the sport of running has been on the increase for a number of years. There are plenty of places to run either casually through London's many open spaces, or more formally with clubs and on running tracks.

How to start & where to learn

One of the best ways to start, if you don't want to pound the pavements on your own, is to contact the Capital Road Runners Club (CRRC). Everybody is welcome from beginners and joggers to racers and international athletes. Throughout the year the club organises major races in and around London. Apart from these, there are regular training evenings (women only and mixed), mid-week 1-mile races and, at the other end of the scale, long-distance marathon training. Despite the name, not all the running is on roads as the club takes full advantage of London's parks, gardens and towpaths to make interesting runs.

For an application form and more details contact the Capital Road Runners Club, 8 Upper Montague Street W1 or Martin Miller: 081-807 7676. Alternatively contact the Southern Counties Athletics Association, Suite 36, City of London Fruit Exchange, Brushfield Street E1. 071-247 2963.

Where to go

CRRC meets at Alexandra Lodge, which is on the south side of Hyde Park near the Albert Hall. In the winter months they also use the Seymour Leisure Centre, Bryanston Place W1.

Hash House running

Hash House running is a non-competitive sport designed to suit all levels of ability. A 'hare' (fast runner) runs ahead of the hounds, laying a trail in flour. False trails and loops are laid. The faster

---

How to start & where to learn

Hash House running is organised by the London Hash House Harriers. For details contact the Honorary Secretary: 081-881 4379 or the Social Secretary: 081-761 5679. Runs take place most Monday evenings as well as occasional Saturdays and Sundays during the day. There are also some special events such as a Halloween run in Fancy Dress. Runners contribute a small amount towards club funds each time they turn up or pay an annual subscription.

Where to go

A seasonal timetable is published with brief notes giving the venue of the run, the time to meet and how to get there on public transport. To obtain a copy contact either of the above telephone numbers.

runners at the front of the pack split up to see which is the correct route, shouting 'On! On!' if they think they are on the right track. All these diversions give the slower runners at the back of the pack a chance to catch up. Just in case anyone is still lagging behind, there are also checkpoints and re-groups plus rest stops during the running session. The session usually lasts about an hour. The runs are very sociable, light-hearted and fun. It is a good way to do some gentle training and forget about the effort you have to make. No experience in running is necessary.

Orienteering

Orienteering is a simple sport suitable for the whole family. Children from as young as ten to lively sixty year olds regularly take part in events. One advantage is that you only need to become competitive as and when it suits you. There are many orienteers who walk round courses accompanied by dogs and young children. You can either go round a course in small groups, pairs or on your own. You don't even have to be fit to enjoy yourselves.

Orienteering is rather like a treasure hunt. You are given a specially drawn large-scale map which will either have a course already printed on it, or you may have to draw it on yourself at the start of the event. The map shows the park, wood or countryside in great detail, showing fences, paths, tracks, streams, ditches, buildings and even small features such as seats or hides. The course is shown by numbered circles (control points) linked by a straight red line. You get extra clues as each of the control points has a description so you know where to look when you are in the right area. It might be a fence corner, path junction or north side of a pond, depending on the nature of the park or terrain.

The control points are shown on the ground either by small red and white flags (rather like box kites) or by a post with a symbol or letter on the top or side. To show you managed to find the control you will need to clip a special card given out with the map or write down the check letter or symbol.

The overall aim of orienteering is to find your way on foot to each of the controls, looking for the best route, so that you cover the course as easily as possible. It is entirely up to you whether you run, walk or jog.

Clothing & equipment

When you first start orienteering you need very little equipment. It is useful to have a sturdy polythene bag to protect your map, and your control card if one is provided. The other essential item is a red pen as it is the colour that shows up best when drawing a course on a map. It is a good idea, if you are going to walk round a course, to be well wrapped up and wear suitable outdoor clothing. Long trousers are essential, even in summer, in case you come across a few brambles. You don't need special shoes as a beginner. Wear ones which you are happy to get muddy, and better still something with a sole that will grip if the ground is slippery. A compass is important when you tackle more difficult courses.

How to start & where to learn

There are eight clubs based in the Greater London Area. Names and addresses of their membership secretaries can be obtained from the British Orienteering Federation (BOF), Riversdale, Dale Road North, Darley Dale, Matlock, Derbyshire DE4 2HX. (0629) 734042.

Small scale events called 'local' or 'colour-coded' events are good for beginners. These take place on a Sunday morning from about *10.00* to *13.00*. There won't always be an event in London every Sunday but you probably won't have to travel far outside if you want to go more frequently. Details of events for the following two or three weeks are given regularly on 071-380 0535 (answerphone). This gives sketchy details and a grid reference of where to find the parking for the event.

The other type of orienteering available all year round and any day of the week is the 'permanent course'. There are more than 10 in and around London. These are very good for beginners as you can devise your own course. You will need a map, which is generally available locally for a small charge.

Where to go

Permanent courses in the London area:

Abbey Wood, Lesnes Abbey Woods and Bostall Heath

Map packs from Crook Log Sports Centre, Brampton Road, Bexleyheath, Kent DA7 4HH. 081-304 5386. *Open: 09.45-21.30 Mon-Sun.* For further information contact Phil Basford: 081-856 6929.
Charge

Barnes Common SW13

Map pack from Barnes Community Association (BCA), Rose House, 70 Barnes High Street SW13. 081-878 2359. *Open 10.30-16.00 Mon-Fri, 10.00-12.00 Sat.*
Charge

Beddington Park, Sutton, Surrey

Map pack from 1) Westcroft Sports Centre, Westcroft Road, Carshalton, Surrey SM5 3AL. 081-770 4800. *Open 10.00-21.00 Mon-Sun.* 2) Central Sutton Library, Civic Centre, St Nicholas Way, Sutton, Surrey SM1 1EA. 081-770 4700. *Open: 09.30-20.00 Tue-*

Fri, 09.30-17.00 Sat. For further information contact Pauline Ward:
081-393 2305.
Free

Crystal Palace Park SE24
Map pack from 1) Crystal Palace Park Zoo 2) Bromley Leisure
Services, Rochester Avenue, Bromley, Kent BR1 3UH. For further
information contact Bob Runcie: (0883) 716781.
Charge

Danson Park
Map pack from Crook Log Sports Centre, Brampton Road,
Bexleyheath, Kent DA7 4HH. 081-304 5386. *Open: 09.45-21.30
Mon-Sun.* For further information contact Phil Basford: 081-856
6929.
Charge

Darrick Wood, Keston Common, Elmstead Wood and Jubilee Park, Pett's Wood
Map pack including all areas from 1) Bromley Leisure Services,
Rochester Avenue, Bromley, Kent BR1 3UH 2) from nature centres
at High Elms, High Elms Road, Farnborough, Surrey. (0689)
862815. *Open: 14.00-16.30 Wed, 10.30-16.30 Sat & Sun.*
Scadbury Park, Grovelands Road, St Paul's Cray, Kent. 081-302
7496. *Open: 10.30-16.30 Sun.*
Charge

Hampstead Heath
Map pack from the Park Office, Parliament Hill NW3. 071-485 4491.
Enquiries: The Park Office, Parliament Hill NW3. 071-485 4491.

Shooters Hill, Woolwich E16
Map pack from 1) Crook Log Sports Centre, Brampton Road,
Bexleyheath, Kent DA7 4HH. 081-304 5386. *Open: 09.45-21.30
Mon-Sun.* For further information contact Phil Basford: 081-856
6929.
Charge

Hainault Forest Country Park
Map pack from Country Park Office by the main park entrance on
Romford Road, A1112. *Open 8.30-dusk Mon-Sun.* For further infor-
mation contact the Country Park Office: 081-500 3106.
Charge

Lee Valley Park
Map packs from the Lee Valley Park Countryside centre, Crooked
Mile, Waltham Abbey, Essex EN9 1QX. *Open Apr-Oct 10.00-17.00
Mon-Sun; Nov-Mar 10.30-16.30 Tue-Fri.* For further information con-
tact the Countryside Centre: (0992) 893345.
Charge

Addington Hills, Croydon, Surrey
Maps from 1) Shirley Hills café on Addington Hills 2) Central Library,
Katherine Street, Croydon, Surrey. 081-760 5400. 3) Parks depart-
ment, Taberner Street, Croydon, Surrey. 081-760 5707.

Rambling

There are many activities organised in London and the surrounding area by the Rambler's Association. For further details see p44.

On your bike

You do not have to be either fit or young to take to a bike. This is because the bike is a highly efficient machine, designed to work for you. Cycling is an aerobic exercise. It helps to develop the heart muscle and improve lung capacity. It will also improve general body tone, especially the legs, but also the shoulders, back and arms. Cycling is a convenient way to travel and will easily beat a car or bus on journeys in inner London. Traffic here now moves more slowly than when the bicycle was introduced over 100 years ago.

How to start & where to learn
New cyclists in London can get help from the London Cycling Campaign (LCC), 3 Stamford Street SE1. 071-928 7220. It campaigns on London-wide cycling issues such as providing cycle routes and improving the roads for cyclists. They also run maintenance classes, and will try to put new cyclists in touch with a 'Bike Mate' who can offer encouragement and tips. They also run women's maintenance classes, discount schemes and a bi-monthly magazine and can put you in touch with local cycling groups.

In addition to cycling for pleasure or to and from work, there are many cycle-related sports which take place in London.

Bicycle Polo

This sport was started in 1891 in County Wicklow, Ireland, by a cyclist who had retired from a career in racing. In its heyday, at the beginning of the century, bicycle polo featured as an Olympic trial sport. Since then it has declined in popularity, but its present adherents are very enthusiastic.

Beginners are welcome and the only qualification needed is the ability to ride a bike. The game is like a land version of water polo. The pitch is the same size as a football pitch with goals at each end. There are six in a team (of men and women), though one of these is reserve. The game lasts for six 15-minute periods known as 'chukkers'. The aim is to score the most goals. The ball is driven up field using a mallet, and is trapped by blocking with the bicycle wheels. Players are allowed to stop the ball with their body and kick it provided it is in the air and the player is not dismounted (having a foot on the ground constitutes being dismounted). Defending players may tackle with their bicycles and shoulder charge, but may not slash with their mallets.

Clothing & equipment
Special bicycles are used in the sport, not just because they take a fair amount of battering. They are very low-geared with no brake, gear levers or anything else that could cause injury. The mallets are made from cane with a wooden head, and the ball used to be made from bamboo root but nowadays is usually nylon. Players need shin pads but helmets are surprisingly not essential. Standard wear is football kit, but shorts and T-shirts or tracksuits are acceptable.

How to start & where to learn
For more details on the sport and London clubs contact Garry Beckett, (General Secretary), The Bicycle Polo Association, 5 Archer Road, South Norwood SE25. 081-656-9724.

Clubs welcome new members. Bikes and mallets are provided but if you take up the sport seriously, you are encouraged to get your own bike. The clubs play regularly during the week and there are London leagues as well as national matches.

Where to play
There are two main London clubs, the Chelsea Peddlers, who play at Hurlingham Park, Fulham SW6 and The King's Bicycle Polo Club who play at King George's Park, Wandsworth SW18.

Bicycle Moto-cross (BMX)

BMX racing takes place on specially-built tracks. Berms (built-up corners), lumps and bumps test the skills of the riders. Races are organised according to age groups and sex, starting with 5s and under and going up to 40 plus. Each race may have several heats known as 'motos'. Good riders can go on to compete in regional and national races.

Clothing & equipment

A specialist bike is needed. These are known as BMX bikes. They have sturdy frames and small wheels. Beware cheap imitations which look colourful but will not stand the wear and tear. It is best to get advice from a club before purchasing a bike. There is also a good second-hand market as younger riders grow out of their bikes quite quickly. Protective clothing is essential - long-sleeved jerseys, trousers and gloves plus a helmet with complete face protection. Some clubs will loan helmets initially for newcomers to the sport.

How to start & where to learn

There are several clubs in and around London, all of whom will organise race meetings, usually on a Sunday. There is a charge for a licence and racing, but it is free for spectators.

Where to go

There are three London clubs:

Hillingdon Club: Contact Scott Dick, 126 Dorchester Way, Hayes, Middlesex. 081-561 4864.

Hounslow Club: Contact Maureen Chenery, 24 Conquest Road, Addlestone, Weybridge, Surrey. (0932) 821217.

Slough Club: Contact Mrs Phyllis Blakes, 15 The Fairway, Burnham, Buckinghamshire. (0628) 602285.

For details of other clubs and tracks contact Jenny Dowson, (secretary), National Office, English BMX Association, Red Roofs, West End, Silverstone, Northants NN12 8UY. (0327) 857945.

Cycle speedway

This is a dynamic, competitive sport. It consists of a fast and furious race round four laps of a circuit either 80m or 100m long. The race may last as long as 45 seconds! Four riders compete either as individuals or as teams of two.

The sport is quite aggressive both because of the physical contact during the racing and the burst of energy needed over such a short period of time. Whilst this sport is open to both sexes, it has so far been an almost exclusively male-oriented activity. You do need to be able to ride a bike quite proficiently and be reasonably fit as this is cycling's answer to sprinting.

Clothing & equipment
You should wear training shoes of a sturdy nature, long trousers and a long-sleeved top. Special bikes are used and protective gear is worn, but these can be borrowed.

How to start & where to learn
There are several cycle speedway clubs in London. To find out about your local club contact the Cycle Speedway Council, 57 Rectory Lane, Poringland, Norwich NR14 7SW. (05086) 3880.
New members are always welcome, just turn up at your nearest track. Clubs will offer practical training on technique as well as several guides and publications about the sport. All equipment is provided to start with. This includes the bike and necessary safety equipment such as arm and knee pads plus a helmet. If it is your first go at the sport, you will be asked to sign a form for insurance purposes.

Where to go
Clubs train on special speedway tracks. Contact your local club to find out when they meet:
Canning Town Recreation Ground, Prince Regent's Lane E16.
Garrett Park, Siward Road, Tooting SW17.
King George's Playing Fields, Jubilee Way, Tolworth, Surrey.
Morden Park, London Road, Morden, Surrey.

Cyclo-Cross

Cyclo-cross is a unique combination of bicycling and cross-country running. The conditions are often quite gruelling as the season runs from September to February. Most cyclo-crossers and their bikes end up covered in mud but still very enthusiastic. Why? As a sport it is a very good way to get overall fitness during the winter. Apart from the benefit of the aerobic exercise, riders learn to be both agile and strong. During the races they have to carry their bikes over obstacles as well as cope with steep ascents and descents.

Races consist of a series of laps usually of about a mile each. A number of obstacles will be included. The venue can be parks, playing fields, farmlands, motor racing circuits. Ideally stretches of different terrain, such as grass, track or woods, are included to provide more variety. Riders are advised to inspect the course first, on foot and by bike, checking difficult sections and obstacles. To do well, it's important to get a good position on the start line. Races last about 25 minutes for juniors and up to 70 minutes for seniors.

Some two hundred events are run each season with races for under 12s, juveniles, juniors, seniors and veterans. A National League competition is held each season as well as National Championships for all classes.

Clothing & equipment

A road bike fitted with appropriate tyres can be used initially but it will need to be stripped of all extraneous items. It must be strong enough to take the wear and tear, but light enough to lift. Clothing should be close-fitting. Long-sleeved jerseys, thermal vests, tights, gloves and hats are essential in cold conditions. Specialist shoes are available, though initially trainers with serrated soles can be worn.

How to start & where to learn

It is important to be fit to participate in this sport, and to have some considerable experience in cycling and handling a bike. Coaches advise serious training programmes including sprinting on a bike, circuit training, keep fit classes and flexibility exercises.

There are many cycling clubs with sections devoted to cyclo-cross. For details of these, and of events, contact: Ray Brogan, 7A Friars Avenue, Walderslade, Chatham, Kent ME5 9PA. (0634) 61943 (after *18.00*).

Where to go

Apart from informal training on suitable terrain, there are several areas used for racing including Shirley Hills near Croydon, Surrey; Elthorne Park, Hanwell W7; Clay Hills, Enfield, Middlesex and the purpose-built venue in London: Eastway Cycle Circuit, Temple Mills Lane, Stratford E15. 081-534 0685.

With water

From the sheer fun of dragonboat racing to serious rowing or the fast speed of the jet bike to a leisurely canoe journey along the canals, there is something to suit everyone in watersports.

There are some very good facilities to be found in London where you can learn if you are a beginner. A good network of clubs exists in many of these sports. They can provide equipment as well as being contact points to meet others interested in the sport. When it comes to venues, London has more than the Thames on offer. There are a great many lakes, reservoirs, ponds and canals that are used for a number of different activities. London's Docklands are also being developed and are planned to offer, by the end of the century, one of the most comprehensive ranges of watersports in Britain. Docklands includes over 400 acres of sheltered dock water (about 1½ times the size of Hyde Park) and 55 miles of waterfront.

Watersports centres

Banbury Sailing Centre

Graves Pumping Station, North Circular Road, Chingford E4
081-531 1129
A 90-acre reservoir popular with local schools and the general public. Skiclub Banbury and Sailclub Banbury also operate from here.
Activities: canoeing, sailing, waterskiing and windsurfing.

Courses: sailing, windsurfing and canoeing for juniors.
Equipment: dinghies, windsurfers, canoes, waterskis and tournament ski boat.
Open: 10.00-sunset Mon-Sun.
BR: Angel Road

Barking & Dagenham Marine Activities Centre
176 Abbey Road, Barking, Essex
081-594 4335
This centre is open to anyone who lives, works or is educated in the borough, plus a 20% membership permitted from outside the borough.
Activities: canoeing (racing, touring, slalom, white water and polo), sailing and snorkeling.
Courses: canoeing, dinghy and life-saving awards, plus snorkeling and polo canoe.
Equipment: open canoes, kayaks, racing kayaks, wombats, dinghies and safety boat.
Open: all year round, tidal water dictates opening times so phone for details.
Tube: Barking

Cremorne Riverside Centre
Cremorne Gardens, Fulham SW10
071-352 1967
Primarily aimed at young people, this boating centre on the Thames has a kayak training pool and six floating moorings. Membership is free to under 21s.
Activities: canoeing, sailing and yachting.
Courses: 12 week canoeing, sailing and yachting courses.
Equipment: canoes, kayaks and dinghies.
Open: Mar-Oct 18.00-20.00 Wed & Thur, 10.00-17.00 Sun.
Tube: Fulham Broadway

Danson Park
Danson Road, Bexleyheath, Kent
081-303 7777 ex3776
This 18-acre lake in Danson Park is administered by Bexley Council. Various watersports take place here including canoeing, rowing, sailing and windsurfing. Each activity is run by a different club. To find out about each one and when they meet contact Bexley Council on the above number.
Open: times vary according to demand – phone for details.
BR: Bexleyheath

Docklands Sailing Centre
Kingbridge, Millwall Dock E14
071-537 2626
A purpose-built centre with 35 acres of water in the dock and slipway access to the river. Priority is given to people living or working on the Isle of Dogs or Tower Hamlets.

Activities: canoeing, dragon boating, sailing and windsurfing.
Courses: canoeing, sailing and windsurfing.
Equipment: canoes, windsurfers, dinghies.
Open: Mar-Oct 09.00-dusk Mon-Sun (quieter in winter months – phone for details).
DLR: Crossharbour

Hillingdon Outdoor Activities Centre (HOAC)
Dewes Lane, off Harvil Road, Harefield, Hillingdon, Middlesex
(0895) 824171
Set in the Middlesex countryside, with a vast complex of lakes in the surrounding area.
Activities: canoeing, rafting, rowing, sailing and windsurfing.
Courses: groups are welcome to use the facilities with their own instructors.
Equipment: canoes, Toppers, Lasers, Wayfarers and three boats for the disabled.
Open: Mar-Oct Mon-Sun; all year round Sat & Sun. Phone for times.
BR: Denham

Mayesbrook Lake Watersports Centre
Mayesbrook Park, Lodge Avenue, Dagenham
081-593 3539
This centre is used primarily by schools during termtime weekdays, but is open to the public at weekends, evenings and holidays.

Activities: canoeing (racing, touring, slalom and white water), sailing and windsurfing.

Courses: introductory courses aimed at youngsters (5+). Higher level dependent on demand.

Equipment: a range of different boats including slalom kayaks, Canadian canoes, basic beginner's boards, children's rigs and storm sails.

Open: all year round for schools; Easter-Oct for the public. Phone for further details.

Tube: Upney

Ravens Ait

Portsmouth Road, Surbiton, Surrey
081-390 3554

Purpose-built residential watersports centre based on an island (the Ait) in the Thames.

Activities: canoeing, rowing, sailing and windsurfing.

Courses: residential and non-residential courses in canoeing and sailing as well as multi-activity courses. Also 'splash days' for young people during the school holidays.

Equipment: good range of craft plus various sized rigs for windsurfing.

Open: Apr-Oct 09.30-12.30, 14.00-17.00 & 18.30-20.30 for casual sessions. Days vary, phone for details.

BR: Surbiton

Royal Victoria Dock Centre

Gate 5, Victoria Dock, Dock Road,
off Silvertown Way, Canning Town E16
071-511 2326

Constisting of 83 acres, this is the largest area of enclosed water in the Docklands. As the water is calm and well-protected and not prone to tidal fluctuations, it makes an excellent learning environment.

Activities: canoeing (racing and touring), rowing and sailing.

Courses: all the activities are taught at introductory, recreational and competition levels.

Equipment: good range of craft.

Open: Varies according to season. Phone for details.

Tube: Stratford, West Ham, Plaistow (then by bus 147, 69 or 262)

Shadwell Basin Project

Shadwell Pierhead, Glamis Road E1
071-481 4210

The project encompasses the seven acres of Shadwell Basin as well as access to the Thames, and is aimed primarily at Tower Hamlets residents.

Activities: canoeing, peacock and dragonboat racing, sailing, sub aqua and windsurfing.

Courses: British Canoe Union and Royal Yachting Association certificate courses for dinghy and windsurfing.
Equipment: wide range of canoes and dinghies plus sailboards, rescue boats, dragon and peacock boats.
Open: Children: *17.00-20.00 Mon, Wed & Thur, 10.30-17.00 Sun*; Adults: *17.00-20.00 Tue, 10.30-17.00 Sat*; School holidays: *10.30-17.00 Mon-Fri.*
Tube: Shadwell, Wapping　*DLR:* Shadwell

Southmere Boating Centre
Binsey Walk, Thamesmead SE2
081-310 2452
Situated in the Thamesmead development area, the centre offers a variety of watersports with the emphasis on the educational side.
Activities: canoeing, sailing and windsurfing.
Courses: canoeing, dinghy sailing, rowing, skulling and windsurfing as well as navigation and yachtmaster courses for adults (through Thamesmead Adult Education) and young people. Also courses for disabled and women only.
Open: evenings Mon-Sun and daytime Sat & Sun. Phone for details.
BR: Abbey Wood

Stubbers Outdoor Pursuits Centre
Ockenden Road, Corbetts Tey, Upminster, Essex
(04022) 24753
247 acres in total including 2 large lakes, a middle-sized lake for canoeing and an environmental pond. Full disabled access.
Activities: canoeing (racing, touring, slalom, white water, open and sea), sailing and off-shore sailing, powerboat courses and windsurfing.
Courses: canoeing, sailing and windsurfing courses.
Equipment: canoes, windsurfers, dinghies.
Open: open all year round but most activities take place Mar-Oct. Times and days vary, phone for details.
Tube: Upminster

Surrey Docks Watersports Centre
Greenland Dock, Rope Street, off Plough Way
Rotherhithe SE16
071-237 4009/5555
Here you'll find 19 acres of sheltered water and organised access to the Thames. Full disabled access to all watersports facilities.
Activities: canoeing (racing, touring, slalom and white water), rafting and rowing, sailing, sub aqua and windsurfing.
Courses: British Canoe Union and Royal Yachting Association courses.

Equipment: a range of crafts, windsurfing boards and rigs, rescue boats and river bus.
Open: Mar-Oct 09.00-21.00 Mon-Sun; Nov-Feb phone for details.
Tube: Surrey Quays

Welsh Harp Sailing

Cool Oak Lane, West Hendon NW9
081-202 6672

This tree-lined area of water is the largest in London. It is an important wildlife habitat as well as a recreational centre. Some dozen sailing clubs use the water. The Welsh Harp Youth Sailing base, open to youth groups and schools, is at the eastern end of the reservoir.
Open: phone for details of opening times for the public.
BR: Hendon, Brent Junction

Westminster Boating Base

Dinorvic Wharf, 136 Grosvenor Road SW1
071-821 7389

Just upstream from the Houses of Parliament, pontoons lead down to the Thames. This centre is able to teach qualifications called the Helmsmans Overseas Certificate of Competence due to its location on the river.
Activities: canoeing, power boating and sailing.
Courses: various British Canoe Union and Royal Yachting Association courses as well as power boat courses, family canoeing and 'splash days'.
Equipment: numerous dinghies and a variety of canoes.
Tube: Pimlico

Canoeing

There are many different disciplines within the world of canoeing, all of which can be learned in London. There is white water canoeing, the down river sport, which takes place in turbulent water of varying degrees, and slalom, which involves dodging in and out of gates on white water. On placid or flat water there is touring, which is the recreational side of the sport, and then there is marathon and sprint racing. There is canoe polo, a form of water polo which is played in short, low canoes with a ball about the size of a football. Canoeing on the sea (or sea kayaking), which involves different techniques, is yet another variation.

Everybody can learn to canoe and progress as much or as little as they like, either keeping at a recreational level or going on to the competitive racing disciplines. There are a series of awards run by the British Canoe Union (BCU).

How to start & where to learn

Novices should start with clubs which offer training on placid or flat water. The general all-purpose kayaks tend to be quite stable and open cockpits prevent you from feeling worried about being trapped if the boat tips over. For more details on how to start, contact the British Canoe Union, Mapperley Hall, Lucknow Avenue, Nottingham NG3 5FA. (0602) 821100. Canoeing clubs are also run in many of London's boroughs, contact your local council leisure services for details.

Where to go

Below is a selection of canoe clubs and centres, most of which offer instruction.

Aquabats

c/o Islington Central Resources
Barnsbury Complex, Barnsbury Park N1
071-607 8362
Canoe club for the blind and partially sighted. Apart from canoeing they do a range of other activities. Meet at *18.45* at Angel tube station and from there the venue varies according to the activity.
Open: 19.00-21.00 Thur.
Tube: Angel

Jubilee Waterside Centre

Elm Village, 105 Camley Street NW1
071-388 3451
This youth club and activity centre is based on Regent's Canal behind King's Cross. Apart from canoeing, there are also courses on climbing.
Open: phone for details of the different sessions.
Tube: Camden Town, King's Cross

Laburnam Boat Club

Laburnam Street, Hackney E2
071-729 2915
Apart from canoeing, this club offers sailing, including off-shore. They also have three narrowboats which they hire out to youth and community groups. Various courses in canoeing proficiency are offered.
Open: evenings Mon-Fri & daytime Sat & Sun. Phone for details.
BR: Cambridge Heath

Leaside Young Mariners

Spring Lane, Clapton E5
081-806 6887
This club caters for 12-22 year olds offering mountain biking and fitness training as well as canoeing.
Open: 17.00-20.00 Mon-Thur, 10.30-16.00 Sat & Sun.
BR: Clapton

Pirate Club
Pirate Castle, Oval Road NW1
071-267 6605
This is a watersport-oriented youth club on Regent's Canal, with a large selection of canoeing equipment.
Open: times vary according to school term and holidays. Phone for details.
Tube: Camden Town

Regent's Canoe Club
c/o Islington Boat Club, 16-34 Graham Street N1
071-253 1246
Open to anyone over 16, this club specialises in white water activities with regular weekends out of London to compete in competitions.
Open: times and days vary, phone for details of sessions.
Tube: Angel

Richmond Canoe Club
Landsdowne Boathouse (alongside Three Pigeons pub),
Petersham Road, Richmond, Surrey
081-940 9898
Open to juniors (11-18 yrs) and seniors, this club organises 'come and try it' sessions and National Placid Water Races on the Thames three times a year.
Open: 18.00-20.30 Tue & Thur, 08.00-13.00 Sat & Sun.
BR: Richmond

Royal Canoe Club House
Trowlock Island, Teddington, Middlesex
081-977 5269
Established in 1866, this canoe club runs three races on the Thames including the oldest canoe race in the world - 'Paddling Challenge' K1. The club's activities concentrate on racing, including sprint, marathon, white water and dragon boating. Many world champions have been members.
Open: phone for details as times vary.
BR: Teddington

Westel Thames Canoe Club
Unit 22, Platts Eyot, Lower Sunbury Road, Hampton
(send mail to: c/o 52 Ashgrove Road, Ashford, Middlesex)
(0784) 255085
Active competition section plus pool training and touring trips. Large variety of vessels. Facilities open to members only.
Open: club nights are Tue & Wed though members are there most days.
BR: Hampton

Dragonboat racing

Whilst this is an old sport, dating back some two thousand years in China, it is relatively new to Britain. A dragonboat is an impressive sight, 40-foot long with a dragon's head at one end and its tail at the other. The oarsmen (or women) sit two abreast. There is a drummer at the prow whose job is to keep everyone in time. At the rear is the steersman, controlling the boat with a single rudder. It is colourful, noisy and can be a lot of fun.

Clothing & equipment
Wear clothes that you don't mind getting wet, especially on the legs. Shorts and T-shirts are fine in good weather. Windproof or waterproof tops are useful. Trainers are suitable as footwear.

How to start & where to learn
No experience is needed to enjoy this most sociable of water sports. The main skill is trying to keep in time with everyone else. Generally after a quick practice session, most people get on fine. The fun comes with racing other crews, usually over a 500m distance. Races don't take long, maybe two or three minutes, but expect to feel quite tired.

Many dragonboat events are organised on behalf of charities with crews contributing a small amount to participate. You can simply turn up and join in as there are often crews who are short of members. However, it is best to get a group together, bearing in mind you need 22 people per boat. For more details contact Merk Hauck (secretary and events co-ordinator), 3 Chess Lane, Loudwater, Rickmansworth, Hertfordshire WD3 4HR. (0923) 770503.

Where to go
There are three centres for dragon boating in London:
Barn Elms Rowing Centre, Barn Elms Boathouse, Putney Towpath SW15. 081-788 9472.
Docklands Sailing Centre, Kingbridge, Millwall Dock E14. 071-537 2626.
Shadwell Basin, Shadwell Pierhead, Glamis Road E1. 071-481 4210.

Rowing

The Oxford and Cambridge Boat Race is one of the most famous rowing events but there's more to this sport. It is certainly not restricted to men, groups of nine, rivers or university students.

Rowing in London takes place on the Thames as well as reservoirs and canals. It is a demanding sport, using the whole body but primarily the legs, back and arms. If you are not fit when you start, you soon will be after a few training sessions! In order to get proficient, training once or twice a week is advised at the beginning, increasing to four times a week to reach competition standard. Recreational rowing is not so demanding. In the summer, rowing training is exclusively on the water. Winter training may include sessions on land.

How to start & where to learn

Rowing is a club-based sport. They normally welcome beginners, provide equipment and instruction for novices. There is always a joining fee which gives access to club facilities. Clubs are usually mixed and offer good social activities. They take part in regattas where there is a range of competition so most people can row against others with similar rowing experience. Anyone wanting to race needs to register with the Amateur Rowing Association (ARA), 6 Lower Mall, Hammersmith W6 9DJ. 081-748 3632/741 7580. There are also rowing facilities and regattas for the disabled - more information about this can be obtained from the ARA.

Where to go

Here is a selection of rowing clubs and centres in London. Most of these offer instruction and help for beginners:

Barn Elms Rowing Centre

Barn Elms Boathouse, Putney Towpath SW15
081-788 9472
A delightful setting on the south side of the Thames opposite Fulham Football Ground.
Activities: rowing and dragonboat racing.
Equipment: large range of boats and indoor rowing tank.
Open: times vary according to seasons. Phone for details.
Tube: Putney Bridge *BR:* Putney

Poplar, Blackwall & District Rowing Club

The Boathouse, Ferry Street, Isle of Dogs E14
071-987 3071
Founded in 1845, this is the third oldest rowing club in Great Britain. Most members are keen oarsmen but the club holds introductory days for beginners. The club uses the Thames as well as the Royal Dock course and has an 8-man rowing tank.
Activities: rowing
Equipment: range of boats, 8-man rowing tank.
Open: 07.00-23.00 Mon-Sun. Club evenings Tue & Thur and early morning training sessions Sat & Sun. Phone for details.
DLR: Island Gardens

Spring Hill Rowing Centre

Spring Hill, Clapton E5
081-806 3097
Caters for 12-18 year olds, though there are opportunities for adults. Beginners are welcome to turn up as there is always tuition and coaching available. Lea Rowing Club for adults also meets here (081-806 8282).
Activities: rowing.
Equipment: large number of boats suitable for beginners up to international standard.
Open: general sessions for young people from 16.00-19.00 Tue & Thur, 10.00-13.00 Sat & Sun.
BR: Clapton, South Tottenham

Trafalgar Rowing Centre

11 & 13 Crane Street, Greenwich SE10
081-858 9568
Also the base of the south-east London Rowing Club, this centre

offers courses in both rowing and sculling from novices to experts. Junior courses in the school holidays.
Activities: rowing and sculling.
Equipment: wide range of boats.
Open: evenings Mon-Fri & mornings Sat. Phone for more details.
BR: Greenwich, Maze Hill

The Women's Rowing Centre
Kew Meadows Park, Richmond, Surrey
081-878 9932
Open to all women who can swim a minimum of 100m. The introductory course lasts 6-9 months but there is a waiting list. Once the course is completed, women are put in touch with appropriate local clubs.
Activities: rowing.
Equipment: good range of boats.
Open: weekends & evenings in summer. Phone for more details.
Tube: Kew Gardens *BR:* Mortlake

Sailing

Yachting is not just for the yuppies. It is a sport that is open to all from as early as three years (under strict supervision) to retirement age. You don't need to be fit, just ready and willing to learn. Being able to swim isn't always a requirement, but confidence in the water is absolutely essential.

How to start & where to learn
There are two ways to get involved in sailing activities in London. Firstly, there is a good network of clubs who welcome new members. They are not necessarily geared up to teach complete novices or provide equipment. If you sail already and want to keep in touch with the sport, it's worth contacting a club through the Royal Yachting Association (RYA).

Secondly, there are several centres which teach sailing from beginners to advanced levels. Centres recognised by the RYA teach a variety of courses from a 2-day taster, very much an introduction to the sport, to a 5-day intensive course. At the end of that, the student should be safety conscious and a confident enough sailor to cope with light winds.

There are special boats designed for children to learn sailing single-handed. These are called 'Optimists'. Adults, who, according to yachting psychologists, respond better to instructions, are more generally taught in a 2-man boat with an instructor on board.

Centres should provide the boat and all the safety equipment you need to learn and if you get a taste for the sport, they can put you in touch with local sailing groups, help you get more experienced and advise on equipment.

There are many centres which offer instruction for the disabled and also a charity set up by the RYA which organises events and regattas for the blind and physically disabled. These take place outside London. The RYA Seamanship Foundation can provide information on sailing in London for the handicapped. The RYA Seamanship Foundation, Royal Yachting Association House, Romsey Road, Eastleigh, Hampshire SO5 4YA. (0703) 629962.

Where to go
In addition to the general centres listed at the beginning of this section, there are some specialised sailing and canoeing centres:

Islington Boat Club
City Road Basin, 16-34 Graham Street N1
071-253 0778
Aims to be a combination of youth club, centre of excellence and community resource for the inner city. The club is mainly for canoeing though some sailing is taught at the Banbury sailing centre. Members' age range is 9-21 years. The Regent's Canal Canoe Club for adults meets here. Purpose-built clubhouse. Good disabled access.
Courses: wide range of canoeing and sailing courses.
Equipment: good range of boats including Optimists and Toppers as well as a variety of canoes such as kayaks and Canadians.
Open: Easter & summer holidays 11.00-17.00 Mon-Sun; other times evenings only from 16.30. Regent's Canoe Club open: 18.30-20.30 Mon & Thur.
Tube: Angel

Kingston Canoe & Sailing Centre
Albany Mews, Albany Park Road, Kingston-upon-Thames, Surrey
081-549 3066
This centre, next to the Thames, is for young people from 12-25 years. The watersports taught here are canoeing and sailing. Instructors are qualified to give help to beginners and all equipment and safety equipment is provided. Opening times are limited as the river does get extremely busy, especially in the summer. For anyone who is experienced in these sports already and looking for a local club, the centre will try and suggest something suitable.
Courses: instruction for beginners to experienced.
Equipment: mostly single canoes, some doubles. Good selection of sailing boats including single-handed craft plus 2 and 3 person boats. Safety equipment.
Open: Mar-Oct 19.00-22.00 Mon, Wed & Fri; Nov-Feb 14.00-17.00 Sun.
BR: Kingston-upon-Thames

Swimming

Hot summers always give a new lease of life to London's open-air pools. The venues are quite varied, from the shaded ponds at Hampstead to the wide open Serpentine Lake and the mighty Lido at Tooting Bec built at the turn of the century. Some open-air pools are open all year for real waterbabies to have a December dip, which is one way of avoiding the crowds!

The Big Splash
Mapleton Road, Wandsworth SW18
081-871 7674/5
This heated outdoor pool has a separate diving area, children's play area and jacuzzi. There are landscaped surroundings and special places to sunbathe. Changing facilities are good with lockers and showers.
Open: May-mid Sep 10.00-18.30 Mon-Sun.
Charge
BR: Wandsworth Town, Earlsfield

Hampstead Heath
There are three venues for swimming on Hampstead Heath, mixed, ladies and men only. They are very popular during the summer so it is best to arrive early. It is very much back to nature with rather murky water and basic facilities, but the leafy surroundings shared with resident coots and moorhens make it a unique experience. It is important to be a strong and competent swimmer if you intend visiting any of the ponds.

Hampstead Mixed Bathing Pond
East Heath Road NW3
071-485 4491
Open: 3rd Sat in May-3rd Sun in Sep 10.00-18.00 Mon-Sun.
Free
Tube: Hampstead

Highgate Pond (men only)
Millfield Lane N6
071-485 4491

Open: 3rd Sat in May-3rd Sun in Sep 06.00-21.00 or sunset Mon-Sun; Dec & Jan 07.30-15.00 Mon-Sun; Nov & Feb 07.00-15.00 Mon-Sun; Mar, Apr & Oct 07.00-sunset Mon-Sun.
Free
Tube: Highgate

Kenwood Ladies Pond
Millfield Lane N6
071-485 4491
Open: 3rd Sat in May-3rd Sun in Sep 07.00-21.00 or sunset Mon-Sun; Dec & Jan 07.30-15.00 Mon-Sun ; Nov & Feb 07.00-15.00 Mon-Sun; Mar, Apr & Oct 07.00-sunset Mon-Sun.
Free
Tube: Highgate

Parliament Hill Lido
Parliament Hill Fields, Gordon House Road NW5
071-485 3873
Facilities are fairly basic but the pool itself is well-maintained. It is a good size, measuring 60 x 36 metres, and is surrounded by a paved area which is splendid for sunbathing.
Open: May-Sep 07.00-09.00 & 10.00-18.00 Mon-Sun; Oct-Feb 07.00-10.00 Mon-Sun; closed Mar & Apr.
Charge (free *May-Sep 07.00-09.00; Oct-Feb 07.00-10.00*)
BR: Gospel Oak

Serpentine Lido
Hyde Park W2
071-724 3104
Situated on the south side of the Serpentine, the sinuous lake that runs through Hyde Park and Kensington Gardens. There are good changing rooms, showers and lockers. Six lifeguards on duty.
Open: 25th May-25th Sep 10.00-17.00 Mon-Sun.
Charge
Tube: Knightsbridge

Tooting Bec Lido
Tooting Bec Road SW16
081-871 7198
Tooting Bec is one of the largest pools in England, measuring 91 x 30 metres. It was opened in 1907 and still has a loyal following. There are basic cubicles along the edge of the pool and a number of showers.
Open: Oct-Mar 07.00-14.30 Mon-Sun; Apr-Jun 07.00-16.30 Mon-Sun; Jul-Sep 06.30-19.30 Mon-Sun.
Charge (free for under 5s and disabled)
Tube: Tooting Bec

Waterskiing

Many people are first tempted by waterskiing on holiday. Despite good conditions they often have a bad first experience due to lack of instruction and lack of time. If you've been put off by that sort of experience, it's a good idea to try one of the courses offered in the capital.

Clothing & equipment

Centres generally provide all you need: skis, wet suit, lifejacket and a boat. Initially there is no equipment to buy.

How to start & where to learn

Tuition involves essential basic movements, such as how to cope when the boat gets moving, getting used to the feel of the skis, positioning the body correctly so that it's not just the arms and shoulders that take the pull.

After a morning's instruction, the majority of people find they can stand up. Progress comes with learning to ski across the wake of a boat, mono-skiing and then slalom and jumping. You don't need to be fit though you will get tired more quickly if you are not. Confidence in the water is essential. Most clubs have courses available for tuition for beginners up to more advanced levels. For more details contact the British Water Ski Federation, 390 City Road EC1. 071-833 2855.

Where to go

Princes Waterski Club

Clockhouse Lane, Bedfont, Middlesex
(0784) 256153
Courses: waterskiing for beginners, intermediate and advanced including morning sessions, day and week courses.
Equipment: three slalom courses and two jumps.
Open: May-Oct 09.00-dusk Mon-Sun; Nov-Apr 09.00-dusk Wed, Thur Sat & Sun.
BR: Ashford

Rickmansworth Waterski Club

The Aquadrome, Uxbridge Road, Rickmansworth, Hertfordshire
(0923) 777418
Courses: coaching for beginners upwards.
Equipment: slalom course, competition boat.
Open: Oct-Mar 09.30-sunset Wed, Fri, Sat & Sun; Apr-Sep 09.30-sunset Tue-Sun.
BR/Tube: Rickmansworth

Royal Docks Waterski Club

Gate 16, King George V Dock, Woolwich Manor Way, North Woolwich E16
071-511 2000
Courses: tuition for the complete beginner up to competition standard in mono, slalom, jump and tricks.
Equipment: mastercraft competition ski boats, 2 slalom courses, 2 jumps, skis, wet suits and life jackets for hire.
Open: Mar-Dec 10.00-dusk Mon-Sun.
BR: North Woolwich

Wet biking and jet skiing

Wet biking is like riding a motorcrosser on water. The bike cuts and corners just like a motorcycle with a suspension system to soak up all the bumps. You need a good sense of balance, agility rather than strength, and no aversion to getting wet. The basics only take a short while to master and confidence comes after a few hours practice. It is possible to take a pillion passenger.

Jet skiing, which works on the same principle of being jet propelled across water, is very similar. Once you've learnt how to stand up you have the freedom of waterskiing without the need of a speedboat and crew. Anyone who develops a strong interest in these sports can progress to race competitively.

Clothing & equipment
Wear clothes that you don't mind getting wet or a wet suit. All other equipment will be provided by the club. There is a good second-hand market for those wanting to own their own machines.

How to start & where to learn
Contact the Docklands Watersports Club (listed below) for all information on how to start and instruction in both wet biking and jet skiing.

Where to go
There is only one venue in London where you can participate in either wet biking or jet skiing:

Docklands Watersports Club
King George V Dock, Woolwich Manor Way
North Woolwich E16
071-511 5000
Open: all year round every day. Phone for details of times.
BR: North Woolwich

Windsurfing

Windsurfing is a little like riding a bicycle. It is a matter of coping with several things at the same time – balance, co-ordination, steering – but once you've grasped it, it all seems incredibly easy. Learning in Britain unfortunately means you have to put up with the weather and cold water but once you have mastered the sport, it leaves you free to windsurf anywhere.

Clothing & equipment

Recognised centres should provide you with everything you need to start (board, rig and wet suit). Take a swim suit, towel etc. Beginners are strongly advised not to spend a great deal of money on their first board and rig. The cheapest in the range are quite adequate and there is a good second-hand market. For expensive gear, you should know exactly what you are buying.

How to start & where to learn

Initially you'll find it tiring, especially on the arms, shoulders and back, so it's best to learn in short sessions of 2 or 3 hours. It is important to be able to swim and to feel confident in water as beginners tend to spend as much time in the water as on the board!

Having mastered balancing on the board, windsurfers progress by learning to sail across the wind, turning into the wind (going about), sailing down wind and turning down wind (jibing). Most centres have tuition facilities.

Where to go

Fairlop Waters

Forest Road, Barkingside, Ilford, Essex
081-500 9911
Windsurfing courses are held on this attractive 35-acre lake. The lessons last three hours with one hour on a simulator on dry land, and two hours on the water. Minimum of three in a group. Wet suits, life jackets etc are provided by the centre.
Equipment: range of boards and rigs suitable for children and adults.
Open: mid-Apr-mid Sep Sat & Sun. Phone for further details.
Tube: Fairlop

Peter Chilvers Windsurfing

Gate 5, Royal Victoria Dock, Tidal Basin Road, off Silvertown Way, North Woolwich E16
071-474 2500
Windsurfing takes place on the 83 acres of enclosed water at the end of Victoria Dock. There's also a roped-off area for practice and a shingle beach from which to launch. The school is particularly busy during summer weekends. One-day courses are taught. This is the location of the London triathlon.
Equipment: good range of boards and rigs.
Open: Apr-Oct 10.30-dusk Tue-Sun; Nov-Feb 10.30-dusk Sat & Sun.
BR: North Woolwich

Rickmansworth Windsurfing & Canoe Centre

The Boathouse, The Aquadrome, Uxbridge Road,
Rickmansworth, Hertfordshire
(0923) 771120
Windsurfing and canoeing courses are held here for both adults and children. Two sessions is enough to get you started with time spent on dry land as well as on (and in!) the water. There is

also equipment for hire for those who can already windsurf and canoe and who are interested in recreational sessions. The on-site shop specialises in watersports equipment. Refreshments are also available. Separate courses for adults and juniors in group sessions (maximum of six).
Equipment: range of rigs and boards for windsurfing as well as basic canoes.
Open: Easter-mid Sep 09.15-20.30 Mon-Sun.
BR/Tube: Rickmansworth

Country style

It is possible to take up a number of sports in the London area that are more usually associated with country life, past and present - the activities covered in this section are archery, fishing and riding.

Archery

Archery, the art of shooting arrows at a target, is one of the oldest sports. It has changed little in principle, yet today's equipment uses modern technology such as tubular steel and plastic. Archery is open to men and women of all ages. Good technique rather than physical strength is the means of achieving success. Many disabled people shoot on the same terms as able-bodied. There are several forms of archery. The most widely practiced, and the current Olympic form, is target archery. This takes place on flat terrain and involves shooting a set number of arrows from known distances from the target. Field archery takes place in rough country, such as woodland, with shooting distances frequently unmarked. In clout archery, the target is flat on the ground, indicated by a flag, and flight archery involves shooting for sheer distance.

Clothing & equipment

Archery equipment is relatively expensive as you will need a basic set of bow, arrows, arm guard, finger guard, quiver etc. The Grand National Archery Society (GNAS) strongly recommend that beginners take advice from a coach or experienced archer before purchasing gear.

How to start & where to learn

For details of how to start, contact a local club or the Grand National Archery Society (GNAS), National Agricultural Centre, 7th Street, Stoneleigh, Kenilworth, Warwickshire. (0203) 696631. There are several clubs in London and many more on the outskirts. Almost all can arrange a course of six lessons covering the basic techniques of 'shooting in the bow'. Courses are led by qualified members of GNAS. A small charge may be levied for these lessons but you probably don't need to buy anything prior to them as teaching equipment is available. On joining a club, there is an annual subscription fee and there may also be a 'target fee' for each shooting session attended.

Where to play

Archery ranges are not open to the public for obvious safety reasons. There are some ranges in London and more on the borders where space is less restricted. For more details contact the Grand National Archery Society.

Fishing

Fishing (or angling) remains one of Britain's most popular participation sports. For fresh-water fishing, there is a closed season for part of the year when fishing is not allowed. This is to allow the fish to spawn. For brown trout the closed season is during the winter months. For coarse fishing (carp, roach, tench and perch) the closed season is in the spring from mid March to mid June.

Do bear in mind that whilst fishing may be fun for those on the bank it may not be so much fun for the fish. Even though most coarse fish are put back in the water, they still go through the trauma of being caught. The National Anglers Council has issued a Code of Practice 'Handle your fish with care'. This includes advice on correct line strength to avoid line breakages and the use of keepnets, how to handle fish once out of the water, and the use of barbless hooks. The Council also recommends lead-free weights to protect swans, many of whom die after swallowing them.

Clothing & equipment
There is a vast range of fishing tackle available. It is advisable not to buy anything before seeking out advice as even the most basic gear can be expensive. (See listing of specialist shops on page 154).

How to start & where to learn
Whilst it is essentially an individual sport, anyone starting off for the first time will need help to learn to fish properly. It is best to contact a local club.

If you fish in fresh water, you need a licence for each rod carried (maximum of two). These rod licences are issued by and available from the National Rivers Authority (Thames Region), PO Box 214, Reading RG1 8HQ. (0734) 535000. Licences run from 1st April-31st March and are also on sale in angling shops. There is a small charge which varies according to category: adult, second rod, OAP, disabled, junior and short season. In addition, you may need a permit (day or season) depending on where you fish.

Where to go
Fishing in London is varied. The river Thames is an obvious area but there are many lakes, reservoirs, canals and small rivers used by anglers. Fishing rights to most stretches of water are owned by individuals, groups such as the London Anglers' Association or fishing clubs. For further information on places to fish and where to get appropriate permits contact the National Rivers Authority. The NRA fishery officers who cover the appropriate area should also be able to give information.

For north and east contact: John Reeves (Waltham Cross). (0992) 35566.

For south and west contact: Steve Colclough (Cross Ness). 081-310 5500.

Riding

It still gives me a surprise every time I see riders in Hyde Park! This sport is carried on in the midst of London and in many of the more countrified spots in and around the capital.

How to start & where to learn

Look for a good school with qualified instructors. There are various stages of tuition; 'on the lunge' is an individual lesson where the horse is led on a long rein in a large circle. This is excellent for beginners. Lessons should go on to teach you how to approach and lead a horse, mounting and dismounting, and then riding at various speeds. Jumping is taught once riders are confident and more experienced.

To obtain a comprehensive handbook dealing with all aspects of the sport as well as a list of recognised establishments contact the British Horse Society (BHS), British Equestrian Centre, Stoneleigh, Kenilworth, Warwickshire CV8 2LR. (0203) 696697.

Where to go

There are a number of British Horse Society (BHS)-approved riding establishments in London and on the outskirts such as the Berkshire Downs and the Chiltern Hills.

Aldersbrook Riding School

Empress Avenue, Manor Park E12
081-530 4648
This pretty yard has a quaint old-world feeling though there are some modern concessions such as a floodlit paddock. There are around 11 horses and ponies available for lessons. They offer basic instruction in riding and jumping as well as 2-4 day holiday courses. There is no unsupervised riding.
Open: 09.00-dusk Tue-Sun.
Tube: Manor Park

Belmont Riding Centre

The Ridgeway, Mill Hill NW7
081-959 1588/906 1255
Surrounded by fields, this spacious yard has a busy, friendly atmosphere. There are about 24 horses and ponies. Instruction in riding, jumping and the British Horse Society Intermediate Instructor's Certificate. No riders over 13 stones. All riders are escorted.
Open: 09.00-17.30 & 19.00-21.00 Tue-Fri, 09.00-17.30 Sat & Sun.
Tube: Mill Hill

Dulwich Riding School

Dulwich Common SE21
081-693 2944
Established in 1958, this school was built by its owner and the instruction offered follows strict guidelines for those who want to ride properly rather than casually. Set in charming surroundings. There are around 20 horses. Instruction in riding and jumping (on client's own horse), and British Horse Society Assistant Instructor's Certificate. No children under 10.
Open: 08.00-19.30 Mon-Sun.
Tube: Brixton BR: West Dulwich

Kentish Town City Farm

1 Cressfield Close, off Grafton Road NW5
071-482 2861
The stables here are an integral part of the farm with the horses housed alongside the farm animals. Although adults wanting to ride do learn here, this riding school is principally for children. There are

about nine horses and ponies. They offer basic instruction in riding with facilities for deprived children in the London area. There is a special farm pony club where children can learn stable management and grooming.
Open: 09.30-17.30 Tue-Sun.
BR/Tube: Kentish Town

Kings Oak Equestrian Centre
Theobalds Park Road, Crews Hill, Enfield, Middlesex
081-363 7868
Riders here can enjoy a canter round the golf course or a gallop on the local cross-country circuit but the school specialises in jumping, which is taught both in and outdoors. There are 35 horses and ponies. Instruction in riding and jumping. Adults and juniors are taught separately and there are also livery facilities.
Open: 10.00-21.00 Tue-Sun.
BR: Crews Hill

Lea Bridge Riding School
Lea Bridge Road, Leyton E10
081-556 2629
This busy school caters for individuals, school groups and the disabled as well as offering full livery and DIY livery. There are around 20 horses and ponies. Instruction in riding and jumping and the British Horse Society Instructor's Certificate. No hiring of horses or unaccompanied hacking.
Open: 10.00-12.00, 13.30-16.00, 17.00-20.30 Tue-Fri, 09.15-16.15 Sat & Sun.
Tube: Leytonstone

London Equestrian Centre
Lullington Garth, Finchley N12
081-349 1345
If you have never ridden before there is an assessment lesson given to make sure you are put into the right standard classes. This large school has some 50 horses and ponies and 34 acres of land. Basic instruction in riding and jumping. Evening classes on Tuesday and Thursday.
Open 10.00-17.30 Tue-Fri (20.30 Tue & Thur), 09.00-17.30 Sat & Sun.
Tube: Mill Hill East

Mottingham Farm Riding Centre
Mottingham Lane SE9
081-857 3003
This school, set in 40 acres of land, used to be on the Eltham Palace estate and was once a dairy farm. Now it is exclusively for horses for lady riders and children. There are around 40 ponies and horses. Basic instruction in riding and jumping.
Open: 09.00-15.15 Sat, 08.00-15.15 Sun, Tue & Thur (advanced riders) 10.00-11.30.
BR: Mottingham

Mudchute Park & Farm Riding School
Pier Street, Isle of Dogs E14
071-515 5901/9271
Set in the midst of the largest inner city farm, the riding school is

being expanded during 1991 and 1992 to include a new courtyard, stables and cafeteria. There are about 8 horses and ponies. Classes are held in a riding arena. There is basic instruction in riding and jumping. No children under 7. No riders over 12 stones.
Open: 08.30-17.00 Wed-Sun.
DLR: Mudchute

Richard Briggs Riding Stables
63 Bathurst Mews W2
071-723 2813/706 3806
Riding classes take place on the five miles of bridle-ways around Hyde Park. Basic instruction is given in riding. Standard riding clothes must be worn for lessons. Evening classes are held in the summer on Tuesday, Wednesday and Thursday. Occasionally there are special children's afternoons for stable management and riding. Phone for details.
Open: 07.30-dusk Tue-Sun.
Tube: Lancaster Gate

Ross Nye's Riding Establishment
8 Bathurst Mews W2
071-262 37μ91
Rotten Row in Hyde Park has been used for horse riding for over 300 years. This riding school continues that tradition and also trains in the outdoor school used by the cavalry. There are 16 horses and ponies. Basic instruction in riding. A number of other activities are organised including a children's pony club where members can learn stable management, grooming and general care of horses.
Open: 07.00-18.00 Tue-Sun.
Tube: Lancaster Gate

Snaresbrook Riding School
67-69 Hollybush Hill, Epping Forest E11
081-989 3256
This school caters for the family and weekend rider. It was established in 1932 and is still run by the same owner. Instruction in riding and jumping. Separate junior and adult classes. There are competitions within the school for jumping, cross-country and dressage. No riders over 13½ stones.
Open: Children: 16.15-17.15 Mon-Fri, 09.00-12.00 Sat, 09.00-10.00 Sun; Adults: 19.00-21.00 Mon-Fri, 14.30-16.30 Sat, 10.00-13.00 Sun.
Tube: Snaresbrook

Suzanne's Riding School
Brookshill Farm, Brookshill Drive
Harrow Weald, Middlesex
081-954 3618
This dual purpose school gives riding lessons to the general public as well as training for those who wish to make a career with horses and obtain professional qualifications. Set in 200 acres of land, it is an attractive brick-built stable. There is a busy atmosphere with over 70 horses as part of the school and some 30 more kept in livery. Instruction is given in riding and jumping and the British Horse Society Intermediate Instructor's Certificate. Juniors and seniors are taught separately.
Open: 09.30-21.30 Tue-Sun.
Tube: Stanmore

Willow Tree Riding Establishment
Ronver Road, Hither Green SE12
081-857 6438
This friendly riding establishment is used by schools during the weekdays and by the general public in the evenings and at weekends. The classes are divided into beginners, intermediate and advanced. There are about 31 horses and ponies, all of whom are kept fresh by regular holidays away from school. Instruction in riding and jumping. No riders over 13 stones. The school has a pony club and junior club which gives instructions on stable management and grooming. There are also special ponies for disabled adults, children and the mentally handicapped.
Open: 19.00-21.00 Mon-Thur, 09.30-12.00, 13.30-15.30 Sat & Sun.
BR: Lee, Grove Park

Wimbledon Village Stables
24B High Street SW19
081-946 8579
These stables are close to Wimbledon Common and the outdoor school takes place in two training rings in the midst of the woods. There are roughly 21 horses and ponies. Instruction in riding and jumping. Evening classes (indoors) on Tuesday and Thursday at *20.00* and *21.00.* No riders over 14 stones.
Open: 10.15-15.15 Mon-Fri, 09.00-15.15 Sat & Sun.
Tube: Wimbledon

On skates or skis

The accelerated motion provided by skates and skis is always thrilling, and very often a lot of fun. Although real outdoor winter sports are limited in London, now that the Thames doesn't freeze, there is some scope to get on your skates, or your skis.

Cross-country skiing

Cross-country skiing, also known as langlauf, ski de fond, nordic skiing or ski rambling, is very different from the downhill sport. It is a question of getting across all types of snow terrain, both up and down hill. Unfortunately in London it can only be rehearsed, but the real thing gives freedom and a good opportunity for a day away from the crowds on the prepared slopes and is also a competitive sport. There are races both in the UK and on the continent.

Clothing & equipment

Skis used are much lighter and thinner than for downhill skiing. Footwear is a light boot attached to the skis with a toe clip leaving the heel free. Clothing is usually tracksuits, sweaters and windproof over-gear.

How to start & where to learn

Snow training in London is limited! However, it is possible to get fit for the sport, learn the necessary techniques and train using roller skis. Roller skis are shorter than snow skis with small wheels at either end and move easily on smooth surfaces such as tarmac.

It is not necessary to be able to ski to have a go at this sport. The best way to start is to go to sessions organised by the London Nordic Ski Club. Contact: Phil Jackson, 173 Nursery Road, Sunbury-on-Thames, Middlesex. (09327) 89849. They have a training programme for all levels and hold sessions at Battersea Park, Richmond Park and Eastway Circuit.

Where to go

There are training areas in Battersea Park SW11, Richmond Park SW15 and Eastway Circuit, Temple Mills Lane, Stratford E15. Country parks are also good areas as well as Hampstead Heath, Richmond Park and Wimbledon Common.

Downhill skiing

For the real snow and the mountains you have to be somewhere other than London! Dry ski slopes are a poor substitute for the snow-covered pistes, but do help those who have never put on skis to get a feel for it. Proficient skiers can use the slopes to keep fit and practise techniques.

Clothing & equipment

Falling on artificial slopes can be painful, so it is essential to be well-protected with thick, preferably old, outer clothing and gloves. In fact, most dry ski slopes will insist that these be worn at all times. The cost of hiring equipment (skis, boots etc) is often included in the admission charge.

How to start & where to learn

All dry ski slopes offer some sort of tuition as well as recreational skiing. It is strongly advisable to take lessons if you are a complete beginner. In some cases lessons are compulsory before you use the slope. Courses vary greatly so it's best to contact the centres for further details.

Where to go

Alexandra Palace Ski Centre
Alexandra Park N22
081-888 2284
Slopes: 1 main slope with 4 lanes, smaller nursery slope.
Lifts: 1 ski tow on main slope.

Facilities: limited range of boots and skis for hire. Private and group lessons available including courses for children. No one is allowed on the slope without supervision unless they have had at least one lesson.
Open: Oct-Easter 19.00-20.00 Mon-Fri, 10.00-18.00 Sat & Sun.
Tube: Wood Green, Finsbury Park *BR:* Alexandra Palace

Crystal Palace National Sports Centre
Ledrington Road SE19
081-778 0131
Slopes: 1 slope including trees for realism.
Lifts: none.
Facilities: good range of boots and skis for hire. Various courses for beginners and improving skiers throughout the season. For practice skiing, book two weeks in advance.
Special facilities: groups of mentally or visually handicapped are welcomed. Instructors for these groups available.
Open: Oct-Apr (phone for details of sessions).
BR: Crystal Palace

Hillingdon Ski Centre
Park Road, Uxbridge, Middlesex
(0895) 55183
Slopes: 4 slopes including a main run, intermediate and two nursery.
Lifts: 3 tow lifts.
Facilities: range of boots and skis for hire.
Special facilities: sessions are run once a month by the British Ski Club for the Disabled.
Charge
Open: Oct-Mar 10.00-22.00 Sun-Fri, 10.00-18.00 Sat; Apr-Sep 10.00-22.00 Mon, Wed & Fri, 10.00-17.00 Sat & Sun.
Tube: Uxbridge, Hillingdon (peak hours only)

Mountaintop Ski Village
Beckton Alps, Alpine Way E6
071-511 0351
Slopes: 1 main slope (the longest in London) including moguls, split into lanes for beginners.
Lifts: 1 main cable tow lift.
Facilities: boots and skis for hire. Private and group lessons available for beginners, advanced and children.
Special facilities: A disabled club uses the centre on Friday evenings.
Open: 09.00-24.00 Mon-Fri; 08.00-24.00 Sat & Sun.
Tube: East Ham *BR:* North Woolwich

Profiles Ski Centre
Sandy Lane, St Paul's Cray, Orpington, Kent
(0689) 76812/78239
Slopes: 1 main slope which includes moguls. Nursery slope.
Lifts: 3 lifts (including 1 on nursery slope).
Facilities: good range of boots and skis for hire. A variety of courses including taster sessions, adult and junior beginners, and general recreational.
Special facilities: sit skis available for the handicapped.
Open: Oct-Mar 09.30-22.00 Mon-Sun; Apr-Sep 10.00-22.00 Mon-Sun.
BR: St Mary Cray (then by bus 51 and 20 mins walk)

Woolwich Dry Ski Slope
Royal Artillery Barracks, Repository Road SE18
081-317 1726
Slopes: slope surface is Delta which is ideal for learning on. It is
being renewed and lengthened in 1991. At present 1:3 gradient.
There is also a nursery slope.
Lifts: Main slope has one drag lift.
Facilities: boots and skis for hire.
Open: 10.00-20.00 Mon-Fri, 10.00-17.00 Sat & Sun.
BR: Woolwich Dockland, Woolwich Arsenal

Ice skating

The relatively warm climate of Britain has meant that skating is
an inside sport and so outside the scope of this guide. London has
a rare exception - an outdoor rink. Staying upright is not too hard,
though if you want to improve it is worth taking lessons.

How to start & where to learn
Broadgate Ice offers a full range of individual and group lessons.
Phone the rink for details.

Where to go
London's only outdoor skating rink is:

Broadgate Ice
Eldon Street EC2
071-588 6565
Around the rink is a full complement of wine bars and sandwich
shops for skaters to find rest, warmth and refreshment off the ice.
Open: mid Nov-Mar 12.00-15.00 & 16.00-19.30 Tue-Thur, 12.00-
15.00 & 16.00-20.00 Fri, 11.00-14.00 & 15.00-18.00 Sat & Sun.
Charge
Tube: Moorgate, Liverpool Street

Roller skating and street hockey

Roller skating has moved off the streets into purpose-built rinks
and discos. Modern technology has made the wheels smoother and
faster, but if you do skate out of doors, look for large, flat surfaces.
Parks, such as Battersea Park, are a good bet.

If you have become a confident roller skater, your skill could be
put to use in street hockey, a very fast game played on roller
skates. Street hockey is a bit of a misnomer. The word 'street' has
been retained in the name in deference to its roots. More than 50
years ago, it really was played in the street. When the sport was
rediscovered in this country about eight years ago, it was apparent
that playing games and matches in the street was inappropriate,
mostly for safety reasons. Poor weather was also a factor. All com-

petitive forms of the sport are now played indoors but some teams train outdoors in the summer in car parks.

Street hockey is played by both sexes and all age groups, starting with a category for the under tens. The maximum number of players in any one game is 12 plus 2 goal keepers, with a maximum of 6 players in each team on the pitch at anyone time.

Clothing & equipment
Players in a match need an approved shirt with an identifying number on the back. Helmets, elbow pads and knee/shin pads must be worn. Other protection such as shoulder-pads and padded gloves are strongly recommended for serious competition. Standard ice-hockey sticks are used and a special non-bouncing plastic ball.

How to start & where to learn
To find out about your local team write to the British Street Hockey Association BSHA, PO Box 567, London SE1 8DB.
Clubs usually have training sessions and welcome newcomers to see if they enjoy the game.

WHERE TO SPECTATE

WATCHING top quality sports events can be hugely enjoyable as well as a way of learning more about the sport itself. London is host to a number of national, international and world-famous events. Below are listed some of these and details of governing bodies who keep track of smaller events.

Athletics

For information on athletics events contact:

Crystal Palace National Sports Centre
Anerley Road SE19
081-778 0131
Within the boundaries of Crystal Palace park, this is the major athletics venue for the United Kingdom. For details of forthcoming events and to book tickets, phone the box office which is *open 09.30-17.00 Mon-Fri.*
BR: Crystal Palace

Southern Counties Athletics Association
Suite 36, City of London Fruit Exchange, Brushfield Street E1
071-247 2963
A useful address for any information on athletics.
Tube: Liverpool Street

Cricket

Lord's Cricket Ground
St John's Wood Road NW8
071-289 1611
Officially the home of Marylebone Cricket Club (MCC) but also an aristocrat amongst cricket grounds and one on which players, both international and home grown, hope to make their mark.

If there isn't a match in progress, enthusiasts can enjoy The Grand Tour featuring the Long Room, the Museum, the Real Tennis Court and other spots steeped in this very English tradition. For details of forthcoming matches and to book tickets, phone the box office which is *open 09.30-17.30 Mon-Fri.* For tour bookings phone 071-266 3825.
Tube: St John's Wood

Oval Cricket Ground
The Oval, Kennington SE11
071-582 6660
London's second major ground and also home to Surrey's county team. Usually one Test Match is staged here during August. Apart from cricket, the Oval is also the venue for baseball and American Rules football.
Tube: Oval *BR:* Vauxhall

Cycling

British Cycling Federation
16 Upper Woburn Place WC1
071-387 9320
Information on road, track and circuit racing.

Eastway Cycle Circuit
Temple Mills Lane, Stratford E15
081-534 6085
Race meetings are held here on a regular basis from February to November and May to September.
BR/Tube: Stratford

Herne Hill Stadium
Burbage Road SE24
081-737 4647
The Good Friday Festival of Cycle Racing opens the season here and the All London Track Championships is held in June.
BR: Herne Hill

Football

The professional football season lasts from August to April. Matches are played on Saturday afternoons, most Bank holidays and some evenings. Kick off usually at *15.00* & *19.00*. Tickets can be bought at the ground. Be aware that new laws are coming into effect requiring spectators to have identity cards and club membership.

The 11 clubs with their grounds in central London are listed below:
Arsenal FC
Highbury Stadium, Avenell Road N5. 071-226 0304.
(Recorded ticket information: 071-359 0131.)
Charlton Athletic FC
Selhurst Park SE25 (sharing Crystal Palace ground). 081-771 6321.
Chelsea FC
Stamford Bridge, Fulham Road SW6. 071-385 5545.
Crystal Palace FC
Selhurst Park SE25. 081-653 4462.

Fulham FC
Craven Cottage, Stevenage Road SW6. 071-736 6561.
Millwall FC
The Den, Cold Blow Lane, New Cross SE14. 071-639 3143.
Orient FC
Brisbane Road, Leyton E10. 081-539 2223.
Queen's Park Rangers FC
South Africa Road W12. 081-743 0262.
Tottenham Hotspur FC
White Hart Lane Ground, 748 High Rd N17. 081-801 3411.
West Ham United FC
Boleyn Ground, Green Street, Newham E13. 081-472 2740.
Wimbledon FC
49 Durnsford Road SW19. 081-946 6311.
Home internationals, international and club championships are held at Wembley Stadium. Tickets can be bought in advance from the box office: Wembley Stadium, Empire Way, Wembley, Middlesex. 081-902 1234, or various London ticket agencies.

Golf

For the many aspiring players of this game, there is an opportunity to see internationals on the fairway.
Wentworth Golf Club hosts the World Matchplay Championship in September or October. Tickets are available from the Ticket Master agency (071-379 4444) or on the gate on the day. Phone the club for exact dates for the championship: **Wentworth Golf Club**, Virginia Water, Surrey. (0344 842201).

Horse racing

A day at the races holds a thrill for many people. There is the excitement of the races themselves, the chance to have a flutter, and good catering and bar facilities to celebrate success, or perhaps drown your sorrows! Today's racecourses have a good range of amenities. Many provide special packages for firms and groups wanting to have a day out with a difference.

The horse racing season is March to November for flat racing, with steeplechasing from August to June. There are five main courses within easy reach of London. All of these hold well-known meetings throughout the year such as the Derby or Royal Ascot. Each course has a list of fixtures and prices published annually.

Ascot Racecourse
Ascot, Berkshire
(0344) 22211
Queen Anne inaugurated racing at Ascot in 1711. From these royal but small beginnings, it has grown into one of the greatest race-courses in the world. Ascot is best known for its four-day Royal

Meeting in June when royalty parade on the racecourse, top hats and tails are the order of the day, and the hats worn by the ladies are watched as closely as the races.

Racing also continues here throughout the year with Diamond Day in July featuring the King George VI and Queen Elizabeth Stakes and a festival of racing in September.

BR: Ascot

Epsom Racecourse

Epsom, Surrey
(0372) 464348

Epsom and horseracing have been inextricably linked for over 200 years since the first Derby was contested here on the first Wednesday in June. Lord Derby and Lord Bunbury raced their horses over the same 1½ miles as the horse race today. The setting is still as pretty with the course commanding wonderful views across the countryside over the undulating downs. During 1990 there has been a major rebuilding scheme to improve the existing Grandstand building.

There are about eight meetings here a year. Apart from the Derby, the other well-known race is the Gold Seal Oaks, a traditional day for ladies as this is the premier race for fillies.

BR: Epsom

Kempton Park Racecourse

Sunbury-on-Thames, Middlesex
(0932) 782292

Kempton's traditional two day Christmas festival is one of the highlights of the year with steeplechasers and hurdlers seen in action in the King George VI. During the summer, the leading thoroughbreds are in action with day and evening meetings. One of the most spectacular is the Racal meeting in June which includes military bands and a firework display accompanying the 1812 overture.

BR: Sunbury-on-Thames

Royal Windsor Racecourse

Maidenhead Road, Windsor, Berkshire
0753) 865234

Set in 165 acres of beautiful Berkshire countryside, Windsor racecourse was constructed in 1865. The 1¾ mile course, bounded on the north, east and south by the river Thames, runs in a figure of eight. Spectators get an excellent view of the racing.

Windsor is renowned for its summer season of evening racing, a tradition established over 25 years ago. Eleven days of flat racing are run between April and August, jump racing is from December to March. All accompanied children under 16 are admitted free to the enclosures.

BR: Windsor Riverdale, Windsor Central

Sandown Park
Esher, Surrey
(0372) 463072
Sandown racecourse has won 8 out of the last 13 Racecourse of the Year awards. It is set in a spectacular amphitheatre with purpose-built modern facilities and unrivalled comfort for the racegoers. Two of the major attractions of the racing calendar are the jumping classic, the Whitbread Gold Cup and the international Coral-Eclipse Stakes in July.
BR: Esher

Motor racing

The nearest venue to London is Brand's Hatch, just a short drive down the M20, but not at the speed of some of the competitors!

Brand's Hatch
Fawkham, Dartford, Kent
(0474) 872331
There is a wide range of meetings held here at all levels of the sport including national and international races. From motor cycles and rally cross to trucks and top single-seater and saloon formulae. Also the venue for Britain's only international round of Formula 3000. Main season is March-October. Phone for full details of all meetings and activities.

Polo

Take a picnic and enjoy an hour of polo in the lovely settings of either Windsor or Ham, near Richmond.

Guard's Polo Club
Smith's Lawn, Windsor, Berkshire
(0784) 434212
The season runs from May to September with polo every afternoon. A variety of teams play. Members of the public are welcome to watch, but should phone first to check details.
Charge
BR: Windsor

Ham Polo Ground
Richmond Road, Petersham, Surrey
081-398 3263 (The Secretary)
081-940 2020 (The Polo Manager)
Matches are played here every Sunday afternoon from May to September. This attractive ground is near Ham House whose gardens are well worth a visit.
Charge
BR: Hampton Court

Rowing

The best known London event is the Oxford versus Cambridge Boat Race which runs from Putney to Mortlake either in March or April, with good viewing points along the river and on the bridges. Other races may offer more to see, however. Regattas are held throughout the year in the London region at Chiswick, Hammersmith, Kingston, Putney, Richmond and Twickenham. For details of events contact:

The Amateur Rowing Association
6 Lower Mall, Hammersmith W6
081-748 3632

Rugby

Rugby Football Union
RFU Ground, Whitton Road
Twickenham, Middlesex
081-892 8161
This is the venue for home internationals, internationals and finals of club, county and divisional competitions. The main season runs from January to March. Apart from attending the matches, you can go on the tour (see below) or visit the RFU shop and museum.

The RFU Tour
Lasting about 1¼ hours, this tour gives enthusiasts a chance to see the turf from the Royal Box and peep into the changing rooms, plus plenty of rugby history and a short film. Tours: *10.30 & 14.30 Mon-Fri*. Contact the Tours Manager: 081-892 8161 to confirm availability.
Ground: *Open: 09.00-13.00 & 14.15-17.00 Mon-Fri.*
BR: Twickenham

Tennis

Wimbledon Lawn Tennis Championships
All England Lawn Tennis & Croquet Club, P.O. Box 98, Church Road SW19
081-946 2244 (recorded information)
Wimbledon is host to one of the most famous championships in the world. It takes place during the last week of June and first week of July. Advance seats for the Centre Court and No 1 Court are allocated by public ballot. To enter the ballot write for an application form to the All England Club between September and December enclosing an sae. Only one application form is sent per address. Completed forms must be returned by the end of January.
To get tickets for the outside courts during the championships it is simply a matter of joining the queue on the day. They offer a good chance to get close to the action.
Tube: Southfields   *Tube/BR:* Wimbledon (then by special bus)

THEATRE AND CONCERTS

Concerts

Broadgate Arena
Corner of Liverpool Street and Eldon Street EC2
071-588 6565
Broadgate Arena is a huge amphitheatre in the midst of the Broadgate complex. There is entertainment here throughout the year and a programme of events attracting people from all over the city. In the winter, the arena is flooded and frozen to become Britain's only open-air ice rink (see separate listing on page 129). From April onwards, the space is used for lunchtime programmes of theatre, dance and music. There are special festivals such as jazz weeks and occasional exhibitions. View the entertainments from anywhere on the four surrounding levels. Bring a picnic or use one of the restaurants or winebars around the arena.
Lunchtime concerts *Apr-Oct 12.30-14.00 Mon-Sun.*
Free
Tube: Liverpool Street *BR:* Liverpool Street

Crystal Palace Park SE20
081-778 7148
The summer concerts, in a similar style to those at Kenwood, run on Sunday afternoons during July and August. There is space on the grass for spectators and the orchestra is sited behind the lake. Phone for details of each concert and for advance bookings.
Charge
Tube: Brixton (then by bus 2A, 2B, 3, 3A) *BR:* Crystal Palace

Horniman Gardens
100 London Road, Forest Hill SE23
081-699 2339
On Sunday afternoons during July and August, a number of brass bands, mixed with the occasional folk group, perform in the bandstand here. During the school summer holidays there are shows for children on Tuesdays and Thursdays. Phone for details.
Free
BR: Forest Hill

Kenwood Lakeside Concerts

Kenwood House, Hampstead Lane NW3
081-348 1286
What better way to spend a summer evening than picnicking in
the lovely grounds of Kenwood House listening to music played by
some of the most famous orchestras in the world. There is music to
suit everyone from well-known classical composers such as
Beethoven and Tchaikovsky to the memorable beat of Glenn
Miller. On some evenings the music is accompanied by a dazzling
display of fireworks. Arrive in plenty of time as the nearby roads
get quite congested and picnic spaces do fill up. Part of the heath
is also roped off for parking but this can get very busy. There's
plenty of pre-concert entertainment to be had watching the rest of
the audience.
Concerts *Jul-Aug every Sat evening.*
Charge
Tube: Archway (then bus 210), Golders Green (then bus 210)

Royal Parks Band Performances

Greenwich Park, Hyde Park, Regent's Park and St James's Park.
A programme of music is put on during the summer months (late
May to end of August) at the bandstands in these parks.
Performances are on Sunday and Bank holiday mid-afternoons
and early evening in all parks, and at St James's and Regent's Park
there is also music during the week over the lunchtime period and
early evening. During July and August there are puppet shows for
children from Monday to Saturday in the morning and afternoon
at the children's playgrounds in Kensington Gardens, Regent's
Park and Greenwich Park.
Free (though normal deckchair charges apply)
For transport details see individual park entries.

Theatre

Covent Garden Street Theatre
Throughout the year there are a huge range of street performers on the Piazza as well as in the arcade. It is pot luck as to what might be on from jugglers and clowns to musicians or mime artists. The more compelling the act the bigger the crowd but there's generally plenty of room to see.
Free
Tube: Covent Garden

George Inn
77 Borough High Street SE1
071-407 2056
This historic pub is the only galleried coaching inn to survive intact. On St George's Day, which also happens to be Shakespeare's birthday, one of his plays is put on in the courtyard in the pub. Seats are provided. Other plays are put on during the summer season on an irregular basis. Look out for posters on the gates of the pub, or telephone for details. Morris dancers also perform here some evenings and weekends during the summer. Good choice of beer, incidentally.
Free
Tube: London Bridge

Holland Park Theatre
Holland Park, Kensington High Street W8
Box Office: 071-602 7856 Information: 071-603 1123
Although officially open air, there is a massive canopy to save you from the worst of the elements if it rains. The summer programme usually includes some opera, dance and theatre.
Performances *Jun-mid Aug 19.30 or 20.00. Phone for exact details.*
Charge
Tube: High Street Kensington

Open-air theatre

Inner Circle, Regent's Park NW1
071-486 2431
Just by the scented rose garden in the heart of Regent's Park is the open-air theatre. The season usually consists of two Shakespearean productions and one other play, either a musical or a modern classic, which alternate throughout the summer. There is no shelter from the elements, so bring a blanket and wrap up well.

Food is served before the show, as well as mulled wine, coffee and other refreshments in the interval. There's no need to gulp it down either as you can take drinks into the theatre with you and the bar stays open afterwards until midnight.
Performances *May-Sep 19.45 Mon-Sat, 14.30 Wed, Thur & Sat.*
Charge
Tube: Baker Street, Regent's Park, Great Portland Street

OUTDOOR EATING

Restaurants

Thanks to the last few years of good summers and mild winters, many restaurants now provide some seating outside. Often this may be no more than a table or two on the street, or a little space under a canopy. The restaurants listed below have delightful courtyards, gardens or terraces where eating al fresco is most enjoyable.

L – lunch
D – dinner
Open to ... – last orders
(Reserve) – advisable to reserve

The price guide in this section refers to the cost of a three-course meal for one inclusive of VAT (and service where applicable) but without wine:

£ = £10.00 and under
££ = £10.00-£20.00
£££ = £20.00-£30.00
£££+ = £30.00 and over

Credit cards:
A - Access, Mastercard, Eurocard
Ax - American Express
Dc - Diners Club
V - Visa (including Barclaycard)

Barbican, Waterside Café
Level 5, Barbican Centre EC2
071-638 4141
From the modern self-service café, food can be taken out onto the large terrace complete with rectilinear lakes and fountains. There is plenty of seating at tables, or the more adventurous can dip their toes in the water. Watch out for the cheeky pigeons. Vegetarian main courses and salads available. *LD open to 20.00.* A.V. **£-££**
Tube: Barbican, Moorgate

Bleeding Heart Yard Restaurant
Bleeding Heart Yard, Greville Street EC1
071-242 8238
This yard features in Dickens' *Little Dorrit* though the origin of the name goes back further – the murdered Lady Elizabeth Hatton returns from time to time to scrub her bloodstains from the cobbles. She now has to manoeuvre around the seating for 40 people. A range of French regional dishes, good fish fresh from Billingsgate and vegetarian fare is served. Music from a grand piano. *LD (Reserve) open to 22.30. Closed Sat & Sun.* A.Ax.Dc.V. **££**
Tube: Farringdon

Le Café des Amis du Vin
11-14 Hanover Place WC2
071-379 4444
A lively restaurant just off Long Acre. Tables are set outside in the sheltered alley making a good spot to relax from the hubbub of Covent Garden. Toulouse sausages are a speciality, but they also offer an award-winning cheeseboard, plus vegetarian main courses and starters. *LD open to 23.30. Closed Sun.* A.Ax.V. **££**
Tube: Covent Garden

Café Kensington
Lancer Square, Kensington Church Street W8
071-938 2211
A charming, modern and stylish restaurant with seating outside in Lancer Square for 50-80. There is also a delightful, triangular balcony with French windows leading to it from the upstairs level which seats around 20. They offer an interesting and varied menu which may include sweetcorn chowder with red pepper salsa, filo parcels with vegetables and ricotta or char-grilled Mahi Mahi with red onions and peppers. Desserts are understandably very popular – try caramel and walnut pie or sparkling champagne lychee jelly. *LD open to 24.00.* A.Ax.V. **£££**
Tube: High Street Kensington

Cherry Orchard
241 Globe Road E2
081-980 6678
One of the cheapest and best of London's vegetarian restaurants.

At the back is their tiny pretty courtyard cum garden. The atmosphere is light and informal, and the food reliable. Unlicensed so you must bring your own wine. *LD open to 22.30. Closed Sun & Mon.* A.V. **£**
Tube: Bethnal Green

Dan's
119 Sydney Street SW3
071-352 2718
A garden at the back of this delightful restaurant opens in summer (from May onwards) and seats about 20. Frequently-changing menu with English and French cuisine such as warm spinach mousse with basil coulis followed by monkfish medallions and chocolate truffle cake. *LD open to 22.30. Closed L Sat.* A.Ax.Dc.V. **£££**
Tube: South Kensington

La Famiglia
7 Langton Street, Fulham SW10
071-351 0761
Friendly Italian restaurant with a pretty garden at the back seating up to 100. They serve a vast range of different pastas, some interesting main dishes such as seabass with garlic and rosemary and classic salads such as mozzarella with avocado and tomatoes. *LD open to 23.45.* A.Ax.Dc.V. **££**
Tube: Fulham Broadway (then by bus 14)

Friths
14 Frith Street W1
071-439 3370
Eclectic Italian fare plus a separate vegetarian menu is served with

style in this elegant restaurant. The menus change frequently but may offer fruit gazpacho, wild mushroom fritters, roast turbot with saffron or Thai fish cakes. At the rear is a small patio bedecked with potted plants, which seats up to 16. *LD open to 23.00.* A.V. **££**
Tube: Tottenham Court Road, Piccadilly Circus

Gate Street Restaurant
10 Gate Street WC2
071-404 0358
In summer tables with umbrellas are set on the terrace outside this restaurant (up to 20 seats). The menu is a mix of French and international dishes with always one or two things suitable for vegetarians. *LD open to 22.45. Closed Sat & Sun.* A.Ax.Dc.V. **££**
Tube: Holborn

Glaisters
4 Hollywood Road, Fulham SW10
071-352 0352
A charming restaurant with a pretty stone-walled garden at the back with hanging greenery and a canopy they can put up when necessary. Wide-ranging menu can mean anything from Dover sole fresh from the market to hamburgers to interesting salads. Friendly, lively atmosphere, popular with the locals. Set menus too. *LD open to 23.45, to 22.30 Sun.* A.Ax.V. **£**
Tube: Fulham Broadway (then by bus 14)

National Film Theatre
South Bank SE1
071-928 5362
The self-service riverside restaurant and coffee bar provides a good selection of salads, snacks and savouries and always a vegetarian ·dish in the restaurant. The benches outside are protected from rain but not cold, although comfort can be had from lots of distractions on the busy river and promenade. Musicians are frequently attracted by the crowd. *LD open to 21.00.* A.V. **£**
BR/Tube: Waterloo

Old Rangoon
201 Castelnau, Barnes SW13
081-741 9655
Spacious colonial-style restaurant with a large floodlit garden and terrace. Varied menu featuring several far eastern specialities such as kebabs, char-grilled pakori and a good vegetable curry. *LD open to 23.00.* A.Ax.Dc.V. **££**
Tube: Hammersmith (then bus 9, 72)

Roof Gardens
99 Kensington High Street W8
071-937 7994
This restaurant is mainly used for private functions, but on Sundays in summer there's a lunchtime buffet for the general pub-

lic. Eat out on the terraces amongst the streams and flamingoes six floors above the bustle of Kensington High Street. *L (Sun only) open to 14.00.* A.Ax.Dc.V. **££**
Tube: High Street Kensington

Gourmet Pizza Co
56 Upper Ground, Gabriel's Wharf SE1
071-928 3188
Set alongside the Thames, there is outdoor eating here for about 40 when the weather permits! The menu consists of pizzas, pastas and some interesting salads including seafood and spinach, bacon and croutons. *LD open to 22.45. Closed D Sun.* A.V. **£**
Tube: Waterloo

Pontevecchio
256 Old Brompton Road SW5
071-373 9082
A comfortable yet modern interior to this Italian restaurant, with tables outside enclosed by box hedges. Brightly-coloured awnings are on hand to ward off inclement weather. The cooking is from Tuscany with an interesting menu and many varieties of pasta which are also worth sampling. *LD (Reserve) open to 23.30.* A.Ax.Dc.V. **££**
Tube: Earl's Court, Gloucester Road

South of the Border
8-10 Joan Street SE1
071-928 6374
The first floor secluded terrace, seating roughly 20, is surrounded by a plant-laden trellis. The menu is a mixture of South Seas Pacific and Indonesian such as rijstafel, tempura prawns or Carpet Bag Australasian (a mixture of goodies!), with a good choice for vegetarians. *LD open to 23.30. Closed Sun.* A.Ax.Dc.V. **££**
Tube: Waterloo

Pubs

In many London pubs the drinkers spill (!) out onto the pavements on fine days or warm, crowded nights. Some places are fortunate to have attractive gardens, or have made an effort to deck a terrace or patio with greenery.

Anglesea Arms

15 Selwood Terrace SW7

071-373 7960

A lovely old award-winning pub with a large forecourt at the front which gets very crowded when the weather permits. Traditional bar food with good, imaginative salads and accompaniments. Vegetarian choice. *LD open to 21.30.* A.Ax.Dc.V.

Tube: Gloucester Road, South Kensington

Anglesea Arms

Crown & Greyhound Hotel

73 Dulwich Village SE21

081-693 2466

Handy for Dulwich Park, this pub has a paved patio with plants as well as a lawn with tables set under the trees. There is a good selection of traditional pub food including vegetarian fare. Sunday lunch is also traditional and very popular. *LD open to 22.30 (to 21.30 Sun & Mon).* A.V.

Tube: Brixton (then by bus 3, 3A)   *BR:* West Dulwich, North Dulwich

Duke of Clarence

203 Holland Park Avenue SW3

071-603 5431

There's been a pub on this site for 400 years although the present one was built as recently as 1939. The best features are the large conservatory laden with plants and the flagged courtyard with Victorian-style gas lamps. Traditional pub food is served as well as a vegetarian dish of the day and barbecues in the summer. *LD open to 21.00.* V.

Tube: Holland Park, Shepherd's Bush

The Flask
77 Highgate West Hill N6
081-340 7260
Named after the flasks which people used to buy here to fill with water at the Hampstead well, parts of this pub have changed little since 1767. Outside is a large forecourt with sturdy wooden tables. Within easy walking distance of Hampstead Heath. *LD open to 22.00*. A.V.
Tube: Highgate, Archway (then by bus 143, 210, 271)

Freemason's Arms
32 Downshire Hill NW3
071-435 4498
Spacious pub on the western edge of Hampstead Heath. Huge garden which can be packed out on fine Sundays. There is both a hot and cold table at lunchtime with traditional and vegetarian pies, pasta and salads. *L only open to 14.30*. A.V.
Tube: Hampstead *BR:* South End

Hand in Hand
6 Crooked Billet, Wimbledon SW19
081-946 5720
Charming old pub which has as its garden the 6000 acres of Wimbledon Common! Food and drink can be taken outside, though it is helpful if the empties are returned. Hot and cold pub food are available including a vegetarian pie and their own home-made Handburger! *LD open to 21.00*. A.V.
BR/Tube: Wimbledon (then by bus 93)

Hare & Hounds
Windmill Lane, Wyke Green, Osterley, Middlesex
081-560 5438
Close to Osterley Park, this pub has a country feel, with its large lawn and views of hedgerows. There is also a children's play area. Food served is traditional fare with a vegetarian choice in the day-time. *LD open to 21.30*. No credit cards.
BR: Osterley

Jack Straw's Castle
North End Way NW3
071-435 8885
Named after Wat Tyler's close comrade who was hanged just outside where the pub is now built. Courtyard with tables and chairs for sunny days and Hampstead Heath a stone's throw away. Traditional pub food in the bar to take outside. *L only open to 14.30*. No credit cards.
Tube: Hampstead

Opera Terrace
45 East Terrace, Covent Garden Piazza WC2
071-379 0666

Opera Terrace

More of a wine bar than a pub, this smart and fashionable spot is near the Royal Opera House, with excellent views of the action in the piazza from the long balcony. Wide-ranging menu which may include goat's cheese and melon to start followed by tuna steak, chicken supreme or a variety of interesting salads. *LD open to 23.30.* A.Ax.Dc.V.
Tube: Covent Garden

Scarsdale Arms

23A Edwardes Square W8
071-937 1811
This pretty pub is in one of London's most attractive residential squares. Easy to admire whilst drinking on the terrace forecourt

Scarsdale Arms

under the plane trees. Holland Park is just a few minutes' walk. Traditional pub fare with an excellent local reputation. *LD open to 21.30. Closed D Sun.* A.Ax.Dc.V.
Tube: High Street Kensington

Spaniards Inn
Spaniards Road NW3
081-455 3276
Behind the large pub is a sheltered garden, part crazy paving and part lawn, complete with aviary. Food served includes four daily specials, two of which are for vegetarians. From here, it's an easy walk to Kenwood and Hampstead Heath or the Heath Extension and Golders Hill Park. *LD open to 21.30.* V.
Tube: Hampstead or Archway (then by bus 210)

Swan Tavern
55 Bayswater Road W2
071-262 5204
A popular and charming pub with a beer garden right opposite Hyde Park. Illuminated from dusk onwards and serving traditional food with a vegetarian choice. *LD open to 22.00, to 21.30 Sun.* A.Ax.Dc.V.
Tube: Lancaster Gate

Waterside Inn
82 York Way N1
071-837 7118
This canalside pub has a terrace overlooking Battlebridge Basin. There is a separate bistro serving full meals. In the bar there are snacks plus a wide and varied salad table. From here there's a short walk to Camden Lock and Regent's Park. *LD open to 21.30.* A.Ax.Dc.V.
BR/Tube: King's Cross St Pancras

Windsor Castle
114 Campden Hill Road W8
071-727 8491
The large beer garden here is shaded by ivy-covered walls and leafy trees. There's traditional pub food as well as a vegetarian dish. Kensington Gardens, Hyde Park and Holland Park are within easy reach. *LD open to 22.00. Closed D Sun.* A.V.
Tube: Notting Hill Gate, High Street Kensington

Riverside pubs

There are many riverside drinking places along the Thames including some of the oldest in the capital. From terraces and balconies there are good views over the river and there's always plenty to see. For a riverside pub crawl, join one of the organised walks listed separately on page 71.

Below are listed a selection of pubs as well as some good spots where there's a choice of drinking places.

The Angel
101 Bermondsey Wall East, Rotherhithe SE16
071-237 3608
15th-century Thameside pub with a pillared balcony giving classic views upstream to Tower Bridge and the City and downstream to the Pool of London. Upstairs is an à la carte restaurant where you can still enjoy the views. Downstairs, pub snacks such as ploughmans and filled rolls are available. Restaurant: *LD open to 22.00, to 21.30 Sun.* A.Ax.Dc.V. **££** Bar food: *L only to 14.00.* A.Ax.Dc.V.
Tube: London Bridge (then by bus 1, 78, 188), Rotherhithe (then by bus 1, 188)

Dickens Inn
St Katherine's Way E1
071-488 1226
Housed in a converted historic warehouse with good views of the yacht marina and Tower Bridge. Choice of food from pub grub to fully-fledged restaurant serving traditional English dishes such as Dover sole or liver and bacon and also vegetarian dishes. Restaurant: *LD open to 22.30.* A.Ax.Dc.V. **££-£££**. Bar food: *LD open to 20.30.* A.Ax.Dc.V.
Tube: Tower Hill *DLR:* Tower Gateway

London Apprentice
62 Church Street, Old Isleworth, Middlesex
081-560 1915
Famous 15th-century pub which got its name from the apprentices

at London Docks who used to row here on their annual day off. Still as popular as ever, hardly surprising given the pretty surroundings and riverside location. Home-made food and salads are available as well as traditional British meals in the upstairs restaurant. Restaurant: *LD open to 21.30*. A.Ax.Dc.V. **££**. Bar food: *LD open to 20.50*. A.Ax.Dc.V.
Tube: Gunnersbury (then by bus 267)   *BR:* Isleworth (then by bus 37)

Prospect of Whitby
57 Wapping Wall E1
071-481 1095
Historic pub whose clientele in the past has included Samuel Pepys and 'Hanging' Judge Jeffries, as well as thieves and smugglers. A terrace overlooks the Thames. Inventive French cuisine from the restaurant and traditional food from the bar including dishes for vegetarians. Restaurant: *D open to 22.00*. A.Ax.Dc.V. **£-££** Bar food: *D open to 21.30*. A.Ax.Dc.V.
Tube: Wapping

The Ship
41 Jews Road, Wandsworth SW18
081-870 9667
This riverside pub has an attractive partly-cobbled terrace on two levels. Picnic tables are set amongst the flower beds and climbing plants. There is a special summer bar in the garden under the hanging baskets. Food is also served outside with a cold buffet table and barbecue, both of which include at least one choice for vegetarians. *LD open to 21.30*. A.Ax.Dc.V.
Tube: Wandsworth Town   *BR:* Fulham Broadway (then by bus 295)

White Swan
Riverside, Twickenham, Middlesex
081-892 2166
This attractive black and white pub has a garden that goes down to the river's edge with ten or so tables. They offer a good range of beer as well as a comprehensive selection of home-made food. Vegetarian fare is not on the menu but they are happy to make dishes on request. *LD open to 22.00. Closed Sun*. A.V.
BR: Twickenham

Pubs can be found along the length of the Thames. Below are three suggestions of where to go to find several drinking places together in pretty locations.

Bankside SE1
Here is The Anchor, an 18th-century pub, and The Founders Arms, one of London's newest pubs, both of which have space outside with good views across the river to St Paul's and The City.
Tube: Blackfriars

Strand on the Green, Chiswick W4
Two historic pubs, the Bull's Head and the City Barge, open onto the towpath here.
Tube: Chiswick, Kew Bridge

Upper and Lower Mall, Hammersmith W6
Just by Hammersmith bridge there's The Dove, Blue Anchor, and Old Ship set along the river frontage. Close by on Black Lion Lane is the Black Lion Pub with its delightful paved garden.
Tube: Hammersmith

Parks

Most parks have some refreshment facilities, though the food can vary from the dull to the dreadful. However, some improvements have been made recently by enterprising individuals offering more imaginative fare.

Alexandra Garden Café
Garden Centre, Alexandra Palace, Alexandra Park, Wood Green N22
081-365 3292
Good wholesome snacks, mainly vegetarian, sandwiches and cakes are served in this pleasant café. No credit cards.
Open: 10.00-16.00 Mon-Fri, 10.00-16.30 Sat & Sun.
Tube: Finsbury Park *BR:* Alexandra Palace

Cake House
St James's Park SW1
071-839 5179
There are more than cakes on sale here with salads and baguettes plus a summer scheme for having food brought to a pre-booked deckchair. Seems very civilised. No credit cards.
Open: Mar-Oct 10.00-20.00 or dusk Mon-Sun; Nov-Feb 10.00-16.00 Mon-Sun.
Tube: St James's Park

Clissold Park Café
Stoke Newington Church Street N16
071-249 0672
Set in the 200-year-old mansion with a spacious lawn, this café offers a range of full meals and home-made cakes (including one for coeliacs) as well as a good choice of drinks. They are probably the only park café to sell Turkish coffee and Indian ice-cream. No credit cards.
Open: 10.00-dusk Mon-Sun.
BR: Canonbury

Golder's Hill Park Cafeteria
North End Way NW3
081-455 8010
This café is set at the top of the slope of the park and the smell of cooking mingles with that of the flowering shrubs and plants. There is some good home-made food on sale, plus excellent ice creams and sorbets. No credit cards.
Open: 10.00-16.00 Mon-Sun.
Tube: Hampstead, Golders Green

Holland Park Cafeteria
Holland Park W11
071-602 9483
Straightforward snacks and sticky cakes are the standard fare here. The setting, just by the glorious formal flower beds is very pleasant. Beware bold and greedy pigeons. No credit cards.
Open: 10.00-16.00 Mon-Sun.
Tube: Holland Park, High Street Kensington

Hyde Park & Kensington Gardens
Dell Café 071-723 0681
The Orangery 071-376 0239
New Serpentine Restaurant 071-402 1142
All these are under the auspices of Prue Leith. There are interesting sandwiches, attractive roulades and a very good value salad bowl at the Dell. Look out too for the small, smart mobile wagons selling drinks and light snacks. No credit cards.
Open: All mid Mar-Dec dawn-dusk Mon-Sun.
Tube: Knightsbridge, High Street Kensington, Lancaster Gate

Kew Gardens
The Orangery 081-948 1825
Open: mid-Mar-Dec 10.00-dusk Mon-Sun.
The Pavilion 081-940 7177
Open: Oct-Mar 10.00-16.00 Mon-Sun; Apr-Sep 10.00-17.30 Mon-Sat, to 19.00 Sun.
Kew Bakery 081-332 1138

Three eating spots in the heavenly gardens at Kew. The Orangery is particularly elegant with high, airy ceilings and simple well-presented food. The other two venues cater more for quick eating. Kew Bakery (due to re-open in 1991 having had a fire) offers snacks, pastries and cold drinks to take away. The Pavilion is a self-service cafeteria set in a spacious building. Decor is practical and food straightforward. The Orangery: no credit cards. The Pavilion: A.V.
Tube: Kew Gardens

Pembroke Lodge
Richmond Gate, Richmond Park SW15
081-940 8207
These self-service tea rooms have a terrace and garden that over-looks the river with views to Ham and Petersham. On sale are a variety of good snacks, salads and sandwiches, cakes and gateaux. No credit cards.
Open: Mar-Oct 10.00-½ hr before park closes Mon-Sun; Nov-Feb 10.00-16.00 Mon-Sun.
BR/Tube: Richmond (then by bus 65, 71)

Ravenscourt Park Tea Rooms
Paddenswick Road W6
081-741 5378
Housed in the old stables, all the food used to be vegetarian but now a wider range is on offer. The inside is unremarkable but out-side there are plenty of tables with pleasant views. No credit cards.
Open: mid Mar-Nov 11.00-dusk Mon-Sun; Dec-mid Mar 11.00-16.30 Mon-Sun.
Tube: Ravenscourt Park

Rose Garden Restaurant
Inner Circle, Regent's Park NW1
071-224 0498
The rose gardens which surround this self-service café are absolutely beautiful, perhaps a good distraction from the rather plain food.
Open: 10.00-16.00 or dusk Mon-Sun.
Tube: Regent's Park, Baker Street, Great Portland Street

Places to picnic

Apart from the parks and open spaces listed there are many more places throughout London where you can picnic. Some of my favourites in the centre of London include: St Paul's churchyard, the heart of Covent Garden; Lincoln's Inn Fields; Soho Square and Leighton House, near Holland Park.

Below are also listed several areas where there's plenty of outdoor eating with numerous cafés, restaurants and bars:

Broadgate EC2
Chelsea Farmers Market, Sydney Street SW3
Covent Garden WC2
Hays Galleria SE1
St Christopher's Place W1

Picnic hampers

To save yourself the trouble of buttering bread or roasting pheasants, there are several companies who will provide anything you need for a picnic. A few are listed below:

The price guide here refers to the cost of a picnic hamper per head: **£** = under £15.00 per head, **££** = £15.00-£25.00 per head.

Boyd's Catering Company
135 Kensington Church Street W8
071-727 5452
A busy hamper business run from Boyd Gilmour's restaurant. All

are prepared individually and they never do the same hamper twice. **££**
Tube: High Street Kensington, Notting Hill Gate

Finn's
4 Elystan Street SW3
071-225 0733
They will prepare any kind of picnic that you desire. Go for a simple meal of chicken drumsticks, sandwiches, quiches etc or the very traditional lobster and smoked salmon. **£**
Tube: South Kensington

Fortnum & Mason
181 Piccadilly W1
071-734 8040
Grocers and provision merchants to Her Majesty the Queen, their hampers can be spotted anywhere from Lord's to Glyndebourne filled with luxuries beyond comparison – pâtés, caviar, brandy and vintage champagne. For only the most discerning picnicker.
£-££
Tube: Piccadilly Circus, Green Park

Hungry Hampers
Gresham Way, off Durnsford Road, Wimbledon Park SW19
081-944 7771
Part of the catering company Gorgeous Gourmets. They offer a range of picnic hampers which may include asparagus mousse, chicken breasts stuffed with fresh oranges, salmon en croute and strawberries and cream. **£-££**
Tube: Wimbledon Park

Pie Man
23 Pensbury Street, South Lambeth SW8
071-627 5232/720 0094
Excellent food for the serious picnicker. You could be tempted with Scotch quail's eggs, Yorkshire puddings filled with horseradish, poached salmon surrounded by spinach and summer pudding and cream. **£**
Tube: Clapham North, Stockwell *BR:* Wandsworth Road

SHOPPING

General sports shops

Astral Sports
D H Evans, 318 Oxford Street W1
071-629 8800
In the basement of the store is a huge range of sports equipment and clothing for tennis, squash, badminton, golf, riding, athletics, dance – you name it.
Open: 09.30-18.00 Mon-Fri (to 20.00 Thur), 09.00-19.00 Sun.

Lillywhites
Piccadilly Circus W1
071-930 3181
A huge store with several floors selling a vast range of equipment, clothing and accessories for many different sports.
Open: 09.30-18.00 Mon-Sat, to 19.00 Thur.

Olympus Sports
301 Oxford Street W1
071-436 7605
Wide range of tennis, squash and badminton equipment, swimwear, ski-wear and a large training shoe department. Sports bags and hand-luggage too.
Open: 09.30-18.00 Mon-Sat, to 20.00 Thur.

Specialist sport shops

It is often worth seeking out a specialist sports shop to buy equipment, especially when just starting out. The staff will usually be able to give advice and information on your sport.

Angling

Acton Angling Centre
187 Old Oak Road W3
081-743 3381
Branch at: 94 Hammersmith Bridge Road W6
Beginners to the sport are welcome to come and get advice on equipment for any type of angling. The complete range of tackle is stocked including sea, coarse, game, and match fishing.
Open: 09.00-17.30 Mon-Thur, to 19.00 Fri, to 18.00 Sat.

Ashpoles of Islington
15 Green Lanes N16
071-226 6575
Good selection of rods, clothing and accessories.
Open: 09.00-18.00 Tue-Fri, to 17.30 Sat.

Farlow's of Pall Mall
5 Pall Mall SW1
071-839 2423
You can get kitted out here for fishing, riding and other country
sports with a good choice of outdoor clothing. A wide range of
fishing tackle is stocked covering all aspects of the sport.
Open: 09.00-18.00 Mon-Fri, to 16.00 Sat.

Gerry's of Wimbledon
170-176 The Broadway SW19
081-540 6773
A selection of tackle is stocked here plus all the necessary outdoor
clothing including good quality waterproofs.
Open: 09.00-18.00 Mon-Sat.

House of Hardy
61 Pall Mall SW1
071-839 5515
Top quality hand-made rods are on sale here as well as everything
for the practical and armchair angler with tackle, clothing, gifts,
books and videos.
Open: 09.00-17.00 Mon-Wed & Fri, to 18.00 Thur, to 16.00 Sat.

Archery

Quicks Archery
Hampton Court Road, Hampton Court, Surrey
081-977 5790
One of the biggest archery specialists in the country, they stock
everything needed for the sport including tournament clothing.
Open: 09.30-13.00 & 14.15-17.00 Mon, Tue & Thur-Sat.

Cycling

Bicycle Workshop
27 All Saint's Road W11
071-229 4850
This is the place to bring sick bicycles as they offer a full repair
service in addition to carrying a large stock of spares and accessories. The summer is very busy and it's best to phone to book
your bike in. Hand-made frames can be built to order.
Open: 10.00-14.00 & 15.00-18.00 Tue-Sat.

Bike Peddlers
50 Calthorpe St WC1
071-278 0551
Plenty of bikes to choose from here plus spares and repairs.
Open: 09.00-14.30 & 15.30-18.00 Mon-Fri, 10.00-13.00 Sat.

Brixton Cycles
433 Coldharbour Lane SW9
071-733 6055
Touring and mountain bikes on sale as well as spare parts and a repair service. Some clothing in stock.
Open: 09.30-18.00 Mon-Sat.

Cycle Logical
136-138 New Cavendish Street W1
071-631 5060
Stockists of Muddy Fox mountain bikes and accessories and also strong, durable clothing suitable for off-road expeditions. A custom wheel-building service is also offered.
Open: 09.00-18.00 Mon-Fri, 11.00-17.00 Sat.

Evans Cycles (Wandsworth)
127-129 Wandsworth High Street SW18
081-877 1878
This large shop sells every kind of bike, plus cyclist clothing, shoes and helmets. They have a wide range of triathlon equipment including specialist bikes and gadgets, swimming costumes and running gear (not shoes).
Open: 09.30-18.00 Mon-Sat.

Freewheel
275 West End Lane NW6
071-435 3725
Specialising in mountain bikes (Ridgeback in particular), this shop also sells all the necessary clothing and accessories to go with that activity.
Open: 09.30-18.00 Mon & Wed, 10.00-18.00 Tue, 09.00-18.00 Thur-Sat.

Mosquito Bikes
123 Essex Road N1
071-226 8841
Apart from a good selection of mountain bikes, plus clothing and accessories, there is also a touring department here with a good choice of bikes, panniers, footwear and touring equipment. If you buy a bike here, they have a follow up repair service in their workshop.
Open: 10.00-14.00 & 15.00-18.30 Mon-Sat.

South Bank Bicycles
194 Wandsworth Road SW8
071-622 3069
This shop caters for the everyday commuter cyclist with a good range of road bikes, wet weather gear and a range of spares to replace worn out saddles and broken chains. They also have the middle to upper price range of mountain bikes, some racing bikes and a good selection of specialist clothing.
Open: 09.00-19.00 Mon-Fri, 10.00-17.00 Sat.

Yellow Jersey Cycles
44 Chalk Farm Road NW1
071-485 8090/6
A range of bikes are stocked for racing, touring and general use as well as specialised mountain bikes and a good selection of accessories. They have a wheel-building service and carry out repairs seven days a week.
Open: 09.00-18.00 Mon-Sat, 11.00-17.00 Sun.

Football

Soccer Scene One
30-31 Great Marlborough Street W1
071-439 0778
An enormous range of team shirts, including all the UK clubs, leading continental clubs and national squads. Also on sale are footballs and other soccer accessories.
Open: 09.30-18.00 Mon-Sat.

Golf

Aladdin's Cave
Press House, Barnstead Plac, Wyvern Estate, Uxbridge, Middlesex
(0895) 33080
Known internationally as the 'largest stocked' retail golf shop in the world. They have every item imaginable that you could possibly need to play or learn about the game of golf starting with the tiniest tee-off peg to electric trolleys, plus a vast range of clothing.
Open: 08.30-17.30 Mon-Fri, 09.00-17.00 Bank holidays.

Golf City
13 New Bridge Street EC4
071-353 9872/3
Everything for the golfer, including clubs, trolleys, balls, shoes and clothing. Half sets of clubs are available for those just taking up the sport.
Open: 09.00-17.30 Mon-Fri, to 16.00 Sat.

Kite flying

Kite Store
48 Neal Street WC2
071-836 1666
This small shop is packed with a colourful array of wind and air toys. There are ready-to-fly kites as well as kite kits, frisbees, boomerangs, and aeroplanes.
Open: 10.00-18.00 Mon-Fri, 10.30-17.30 Sat.

Mountaineering, camping and skiing

Adventure Shops
14-16 Southampton Street WC2
071-836 8541
This large shop has a comprehensive range of equipment for climbing, skiing, camping and survival. Also a good range of books and maps and an outdoor holiday travel department.
Open: 09.30-18.00 Mon-Tue, 10.00-18.00 Wed & Fri, 10.00-19.30 Thur, 09.00-18.00 Sat.

Alpine Sports
456-458 Strand WC2
071-839 5161
Branch at: 215 Kensington High Street W8
The whole gamut of outdoor equipment is here for skiing, climbing, mountaineering and camping. In the summer, general sports gear is also on sale.
Open: 10.00-17.00 Mon-Fri, to 18.00 Sat.

Blacks Camping & Leisure
53 Rathbone Place W1
071-636 6645
Renowned specialists in camping, climbing and mountaineering equipment. They also sell a full range of skis and ski clothing and accessories.
Open: 09.30-18.00 Mon-Fri, to 17.30 Sat.

Camping Centre
44-48 Birchington Road NW6
071-328 2166

All sorts of camping equipment and backpacking gear is on sale here including a large range of tents and trailer tents.
Open: 09.30-17.30 Mon-Sat, (Apr-Sep only) 10.00-16.00 Sun.

Camping & Outdoor Centre
27 Buckingham Palace Road SW1
071-834 6007
As well as being the Scout shop, selling uniforms and handy gadgets, there is also a range of camping equipment from tents to billy cans, plus rucksacks and other gear for backpacking.
Open: 09.30-17.30 Mon, 09.00-17.00 Tue-Sat.

Ellis Brigham
30 Southampton Street WC2
071-240 9577
This large specialist ski shop has a full range of equipment and clothing as well as a ski repair service. There is also a climbing department, plenty of backpacking gear, survival equipment and waterproofs. In the summer, surf wear is also on sale.
Open: 09.30-18.00 Mon, Wed, Fri & Sat, 10.00-18.00 Tue, 09.30-20.00 Thur.

The Rock Barn & The Ski Barn
20-22 Camden High Street NW1
071-387 4068
These two adjacent shops sell a good range of equipment , clothing and accessories for skiing, climbing, backpacking and walking.
Open: 10.00-18.00 Mon-Sat, to 19.00 Thur; from mid Dec-Mar 12.00-16.00 Sun.

Ski 47
41 North End Road W14
071-602 4820
A good range of ski and wind-surfing equipment on sale. Larger and more expensive items such as roof racks and snow chains are available for hire.
Open: 09.30-18.30 Mon-Wed, to 19.00 Thur & Fri, to 18.00 Sat, 10.00-17.00 Sun.

Snow & Rock
188 Kensington High Street W8
071-937 0872
This shop specialises in skis and ski clothing including a range of gear suitable for children. They also stock mountaineering equipment and some tents.
Open: 10.00-19.00 Mon-Fri, 09.00-18.00 Sat; Nov-Easter 11.00-17.00 Sun.

Riding

Bernard Weatherill
8 Saville Row W1
071-734 6905
Bespoke tailors specialising in riding wear and one of the few remaining firms who make ladies and gentlemen's breeches.
Open: 09.00-17.30 Mon-Fri.

W H Gidden
15D Clifford Street W1
071-734 2788
Famous for their saddlery, this shop stocks everything for the horse and rider including tack, clothing and accessories.
Open: 09.00-17.15 Mon-Fri, 10.00-15.00 Sat.

Running and walking

James Taylor & Son
4 Paddington Street W1
071-935 4149
As well as specialising in hand-made shoes, this firm also offer several other services to give comfort to your feet. There are shock absorbent heels for pavement pounding, moulded insoles and specific foot-friendly shoes designed to massage feet using the principles of reflexology.
Open: 09.00-17.30 Mon-Fri, 10.00-13.00 first Sat of each month.

Run & Become, Become & Run
42 Palmer Street SW1
071-222 1314
This shop stocks a comprehensive range of running shoes and

clothing. The staff, who are runners themselves, are able to give advice on what shoes are suitable for different running needs and will assist in getting a correct fit which may help to prevent injuries.

Open: 09.00-18.00 Mon-Wed, Fri & Sat, 09.00-20.30 Thur.

Runners Need

34 Parkway NW1

071-267 7525

A small shop stocked with shoes and clothing for runners. Also a good information point on running events around London, running clubs etc.

Open: 10.00-18.30 Mon-Fri, 09.00-18.00 Sat.

Sailing

Arthur Beale

194 Shaftesbury Avenue WC2

071-836 9034

Excellent small yacht chandler with a special interest in ropes. Nautical clothing, life jackets and books stocked.

Open: 09.30-18.00 Mon-Fri, to 13.00 Sat.

Captain O.M. Watts

45 Albermarle Street W1

071-493 4633

This world-famous yacht chandlers sells a complete range of equipment and accessories from inflatable boats and navigational equipment to clothing and gifts for the nautically minded.

Open: 09.00-18.00 Mon-Sat, to 19.00 Thur, to 17.00 Sat.

Force 4

30 Bressenden Place SW1

071-828 3900

A full range of yachting equipment is stocked including inflatable dinghies, charts, books and clothing.

Open: 08.30-18.00 Mon-Fri, to 19.00 Thur, 09.00-16.00 Sat.

London Yacht Centre

13 Artillery Lane E1

071-247 0521

This shop stocks a wide range of boating equipment, plus safety gear and clothing as well as yachting books. They also offer a world-wide mail order service.

Open: 09.00-17.30 Mon-Fri.

Thomas Foulkes

6a Sansom Road (off Lansdowne Road), Leytonstone E11

081-539 5084

A good selection of all types of gear and equipment.

Open: 09.00-17.30 Mon-Fri, to 16.00 Sat.

Skating

Skate Attack
95 Highgate Road NW5
071-267 6961
All types of skating equipment sold including roller skates, ice skates, ice hockey gear, skateboards and clothing.
Open: 10.00-18.00 Mon-Fri, 09.00-18.00 Sat.

Slam City Skates
16 Neal's Yard
071-240 0928
Branch at: 130 Talbot Road W11
Specialists in skateboarding plus all the associated gear such as T-shirts, shoes and snow boards. It's a good place to come for information on events and where to skate.
Open: 10.00-18.30 Mon-Sat.

Streatham Skates
2 Hopton Parade, Streatham High Road SW16
081-677 8747
Specialists in skating equipment including ice skating and ice hockey, roller skating and the latest roller skate designs called roller blades and Bauer rollers. They also sell a full range of clothing and protective gear.
Open: 11.30-17.30 Mon-Sat (to 20.00 Fri), 13.00-15.00 Sun.

Windsurfing

Activ
557-561 Battersea Park Road SW11
071-223 2590
Specialists in windsurfing equipment with boards and clothing as well as skis and mountain bikes.
Open: 09.30-18.00 Tue, Wed & Fri, 10.00-20.00 Thur, 09.30-17.00 Sat.

Windsurfer's World
312 King Street W6
081-994 6769
Everything you need for windsurfing and surfing including boards, sails and wetsuits. Also snow-skiing equipment and clothing.
Open: 09.30-18.00 Mon-Sat.

Markets

Small stalls and pavement shops abound in London, but the bigger markets have atmosphere, bargains if you're lucky and know what to look for, and pickpockets if you don't watch out. It pays to be early and sceptical about some of the prices, but you need to be skilled to get any big reduction.

Many of London's high streets have food markets. If you are buying food or perishable items it is worth checking them carefully first; once you become a regular it's easy to get to know the stalls you like best.

Bermondsey & New Caledonian Market
Between Tower Bridge Road and Bermondsey Street SE1
An early start makes you a serious buyer, mixing with the collectors and the dealers at this established antique market. Even if you're only a browser, there's plenty to fascinate.
Open: 05.00-12.00 Fri.
Tube: London Bridge

Berwick Street Market W1

This lively market in the heart of Soho was officially recognised in 1892. It is an excellent place to get good value fruit and vegetables, and some bargains to be had at the end of the day. As well as all the standard produce, there are many unusual salad ingredients, tropical fruits and fresh herbs. The more exotic tends to be in the part nearest Shaftesbury Avenue. It's a noisy place with stall holders shouting out their prices above the general London hubbub.
Open: 09.00-17.00 Mon-Fri.
Tube: Piccadilly Circus

Brick Lane Market E1

A haunt of mine on Sundays in the seventies and not much has changed. There's still an amazing mixture of items from old 78s to modern Walkmans, second-hand furniture and silver. Don't miss the traditional bagel shops.
Open: 05.00-14.00 Sun.
Tube: Aldgate East

Camden & Camden Lock Markets NW1

Camden is famous for its markets, the oldest and best known being alongside the canal at Camden Lock. The whole area is worth exploring though as there is plenty to see and buy.

From Camden Town tube station (the best way to travel as parking is very restricted) walk north. First on the left is Inverness Street market which has good value fruit and veg and on the right is Camden Market selling clothes, records and jewellery. Beyond, over the canal, is Camden Lock with a mixture of antiques and modern crafts and the Roof Market. The Canal Market (bric à brac, arts, crafts, and books) is on the opposite side of the road. Beyond are the arches where mainly second-hand clothes are sold, and further up along Chalk Farm Road is Chalk Farm Market and the Old Stables with second-hand goods and antiques.
Open: 08.00-18.00 Sat & Sun (Inverness Street open 09.00-13.00 Mon-Sat).
Tube: Camden Town

Camden Passage Market

Islington High Street N1
Not to be confused with Camden (see above) as this market is in an entirely different area, a bit more up-market and a lot more expensive. A mixture of shops and stalls with a wide range of antique and period goods, prints, pictures, clothes and clocks.
Open: 08.00-16.00 Wed & Sat.
Tube: Angel

Columbia Road Market E2

David Gentleman featured this colourful market in one of his watercolours of London. The whole space is taken over with a

mass of plants, flowers and foliage all packed together and providing not only a pretty sight but a gorgeous smell.
Open: 08.00-13.00 Sun.
Tube: Old Street

Covent Garden Market WC2

Until 1974, this was the site of London's principal wholesale fruit and vegetable market. When it moved to less romantic surroundings in Nine Elms, there was the inevitable struggle between the developers and those who wanted the area to survive. Survive it did, and now the central Piazza and all the radiating streets and alleyways are a giant Aladdin's cave with something interesting in every corner.

The main market, known as the Apple Market, is in the centre of the Piazza. On Mondays, there is an antique market, whilst during the rest of the week the stalls are full of original high-class imaginative crafts, clothes and jewellery. Some items are pricey but it is possible to find very affordable presents.
Open: 10.00-17.00 Mon-Sat.
Tube: Covent Garden

Leather Lane Market EC1

Stalls at Leather Lane sell a variety of goods from bedding and bike parts to paperbacks and plants, but there's not much sign of leather these days.

Open: 11.00-15.00 Mon-Fri.

Tube: Chancery Lane, Farringdon Street

Petticoat Lane Market E1

Rather confusingly Petticoat Lane does not exist, but it is the name of the market held on Sundays in the cluster of streets radiating from Middlesex Street. The road was originally called Peticote Lane, probably after the dealers in old clothes who had their businesses here in the early 1600s. Towards the end of that century, Huguenot weavers and Jewish traders moved in, establishing a large market for cloth and clothing. When the area was renamed, the old name remained. In Victorian times, a large variety of goods was sold and, despite constant objections, trading takes place on a Sunday, eventually made legal by an act of Parliament in 1936. Today, the place is as lively and busy as ever. Clothing is what is mainly on sale but there are some stalls selling toys, toiletries, stereos and other luxury new goods.

Open: 09.00-14.00 Sun.

Tube: Aldgate, Aldgate East, Liverpool Street

Portobello Market

Portobello Road W11

The first dealers here were gypsies buying and selling horses as well as fresh herbs. Now this market, which stretches the entire length of the road, is well-known for a much wider range of goods. An enormous amount of second-hand junk and bric-à-brac is sold and there are antiques stalls on a Saturday. There's also a good selection of fruit and vegetables during the week.

Open: Fruit and vegetables: *08.00-17.00 Mon-Wed, Fri & Sat, 08.00-13.00 Thur;* General: *08.00-15.00 Fri, 08.00-17.00 Sat;* Antiques: *08.00-17.00 Sat.*

Tube: Notting Hill Gate, Ladbroke Grove

Shepherd's Bush Market

Uxbridge Road W12

Vast numbers of stalls and lock-ups alongside the railway arcade. There's cheap household stuff, clothes and cassettes and an interesting range of food with a West Indian bias.

Open: 09.30-17.00 Mon-Sat.

Tube: Goldhawk Road, Shepherd's Bush

Whitechapel Market

Whitechapel Road E1

Sprawling along Whitechapel Road, Whitechapel Market was once

one of the largest Victorian street markets selling a variety of things such as rat traps, cutlery, flowers and skittles. The rat traps may have gone but the range of goods remains as large as ever.
Open: 08.30-17.00 Mon-Sat.
Tube: Whitechapel

CAMPING

THERE are several camping sites around London for those wanting somewhere cheap to stay. There is some choice of amenities, site style and adjacent sports facilities.

Abbey Wood Caravan Club Site
Federation Road, Abbey Wood SE2
081-310 2233
This site provides grass pitches for tents as well as hard-standing for caravans and frame tents in cleared areas of woodland. Advance booking is necessary over Easter and Bank holidays as well as during July and August. Arrivals after *22.00* must go to the late arrivals park.
Facilities: shower and toilet block, laundry and ironing room, telephones, play area and on-site shop.
Open: all year round.

Crystal Palace Caravan Club
Crystal Palace Parade, Crystal Palace Park SE19
081-778 7155
This site maintains that it's the highest in London, with good views from the terraces towards the south. There is hard-standing for caravans as well as some grass pitches for both tents and caravans. It is set in landscaped parkland in one corner of Crystal Palace Park.
Facilities: shower and toilet block, disabled room, laundry room.
Open: all year round.

Eastway Sport & Leisure Centre
Temple Mills Lane, Stratford E15
081-534 6085/519-0017
This camping centre is just four miles from the centre of London. Set in 40 acres of landscaped parkland it is more than just a campsite. Many sports facilities are on hand including squash and badminton, table tennis and netball as well as the Eastway Cycle Centre (see separate listing on page 102).
Facilities: shower and toilet block, telephones, café, restaurant, local shop.
Open: all year round.

Hackney Camping
Millfields Road E5
081-985 7656
Close to central London, this site provides individual pitches for tents.
Facilities: showers, toilets, baggage store, shop and snack bar.
Open: mid Jun-25 Aug.

Picketts Lock
Picketts Lock Lane, Edmonton N9
081-803 4756
This site provides hard-standing for caravans and grass pitches for campers. The sports facilities at Picketts Lock, one of the largest leisure centres in the country, are on hand.
Facilities: shower and toilet block, laundry, on-site shop, telephones.
Open: all year round.

Riverside Mobile Homes & Touring Park
Thorney Mill Road, West Drayton, Middlesex
(0895) 446520
This is a site for touring caravans only (no camping). It is essential to book in advance and pay on arrival (no credit cards or cheques).
Facilities: water and electricity, small shop, shower and toilet block.
Open: all year around.

Tent City
Old Oak Common Lane, Acton W3
081-743 5708
This site comprises shared accommodation in large tents or pitches for smaller tents.
Facilities: showers, toilets, baggage store and snack bar.
Open: 24 hours Jun-mid Sep.

INDEX